Pyramide 2

Students' Book

Colin Asher

David Webb

Stanley Thornes (Publishers) Ltd

First published in 1992 by
Stanley Thornes (Publishers) Ltd
Old Station Drive
Leckhampton
CHELTENHAM GL53 0DN

British Library Cataloguing in Publication Data

Asher, Colin
    Pyramide: 2. Students' Book
    I. Title   II. Webb, David
    448
    ISBN 0–7487–1301–8

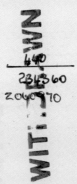

Typeset by Tech-Set, Gateshead, Tyne & Wear
Printed and bound in Singapore by Singapore National Printers

Preface

By now, you know quite a lot of French, and should be able to talk about everyday things with a French-speaking person. You can introduce yourself, say where you live, tell people what you like and don't like, buy things in shops, find your way around a town in a French-speaking country, and so on. In fact, you should feel quite at home in several European countries.

Now that lots of people go to Europe for their holidays and on business, speaking another language is a real necessity. By the time you reach the end of Book 2, you'll be even more confident when dealing with French speakers, whether you meet them here or in their own country. You'll know more about everyday life in France, too, and should be able to cope easily with things like buying clothes, ordering something to eat and drink and getting help at a chemist's.

If you haven't had a chance yet to visit a French-speaking country, this may be the year when you are able to do so. Even a short trip to a Channel port will show you that what you are learning really works!

Bon voyage et bonne chance!

Colin Asher and David Webb

Contents

Unité 1

En avant, la Rentrée!

This unit will give you the chance to revise some of the things you already know.

Also, you'll find out what it's like going back to school in France, and you'll learn

- how to say you're nearly thirteen
- how to say you like something a lot ... or not very much.

la rentrée! EN MUSIQUE !

RADIO K7
THOMSON MRK 324 T
Stéréo, PO-GO-FM arrêt automatique, micro incor-poré
Indicateur stéréo en FM
Piles secteur
Garantie 1 an ....

CHAINE HIFI

699 F

champion Super classe!

la rentrée!

jusqu'au 30 août

O.K. pour la rentrée
les crayons
les calculatrices
les sacs, la papeterie, les accessoires

Pour la rentrée

ECONOM
LE PLAISIR D

RENTRÉE "SUPER"

LES MAROQUINIER DE PARIS
5. PLACE BOSSUET · DIJON
Angle rue Piron
SERVICE APRES-VENTE ASS

La rentrée scolaire, la rentrée des classes, or more simply la Rentrée is an important event in the French calendar: it is the beginning of the new school year, when pupils go back to school after the long summer break. Shops and supermarkets use the weeks leading up to la Rentrée as a time to boost sales. Things you need for school are advertised everywhere, just as they are in this country, but so is a range of household items which have nothing to do with the new school term. La Rentrée is everywhere!

PROMOTION « LYCÉE »
CARTABLE CUIR 36 cm
SPÉCIAL CLASSEUR

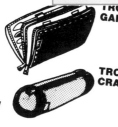

TROUSSE GARNIE

TROUSS CRAYON

TROUSSE CRAYONS
72F

C'EST EN TISSU
ENDUIT DE GOMME LISSE.
(PVC SUR CEL... RME)

du 21 au 28 Août

MUSETTE TOILE KAKI
2 poches
13.95 F

GIBECIÈRE VINYL 35 cm
30.15 F

FOURRE-TOUT TOILE
5.85 F

CAHIER DE TEXTES
120 pages petit format
3.30 F

BOITE PEINTURE
4.30 F

LOT 1 ARDOISE
4.05 F

CAHIER DE TEXTES

Rentrée des Prix

UE CHOIX!

UPER

DISPORT
UNE RENTREE
AVEC DU PUNCH

7

En cinquième

Madame Massot

Au Collège La Guérinière...

It's the new school year at the Collège La Guérinière in Caen and the pupils from **sixième** have all moved up a class, to **cinquième**. A teacher, Madame Massot, is checking details.

She wants to know

- what her pupils' names are
- how old they are
- where they live
- which class they're in.

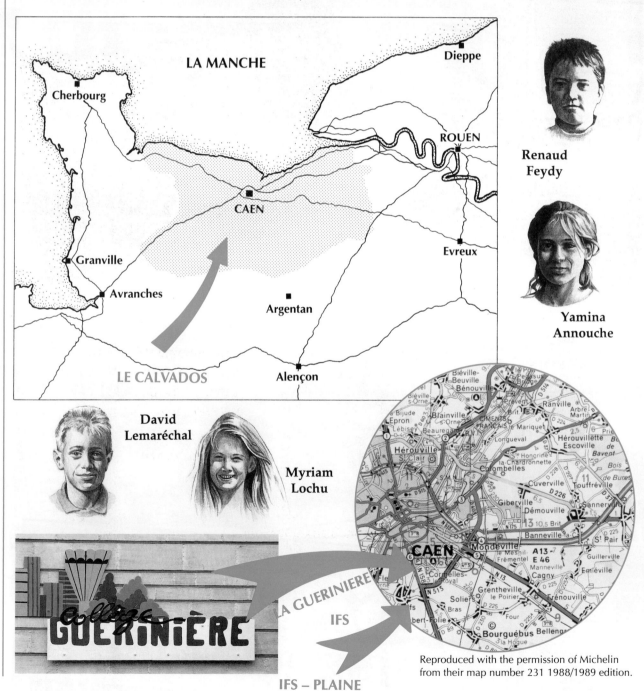

Renaud Feydy

Yamina Annouche

David Lemaréchal

Myriam Lochu

Reproduced with the permission of Michelin from their map number 231 1988/1989 edition.

1 Ecoutez

a D'abord, dessine cette grille et copie les renseignements sur David:

nom	David Lemaréchal	Myriam Lochu	Renaud Feydy	Yamina Annouche
âge	nearly 13			
domicile	Ifs			
classe	5ᵉ			

b Ecoute les quatre interviews.
Note en anglais les renseignements sur Myriam, Renaud et Yamina.

Mots-clés 1

To say your name, you can use as well as	**Je me nomme (Myriam).** **Je m'appelle (Myriam).**
'I'm nearly thirteen' is	**Je vais avoir treize ans.** (I'm going to be thirteen.)
'Near (Caen)' is or	**près de (Caen)** **proche de (Caen)**

2 Répondez

Maintenant, réponds aux questions de Madame Massot!

Quelles matières?

1 Lisez

Voici des étiquettes autocollantes offertes à ses lecteurs par le magazine OKAPI. Les élèves vont coller les étiquettes sur leurs cahiers de textes...

a Quelles matières sont représentées?

b Ces matières ne sont pas représentées!

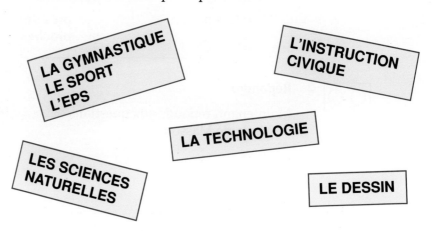

LA GYMNASTIQUE
LE SPORT
L'EPS

L'INSTRUCTION
CIVIQUE

LA TECHNOLOGIE

LES SCIENCES
NATURELLES

LE DESSIN

c Dessine un autocollant pour une de ces matières.

d *Et toi!*

- Est-ce que tu aimes les maths?
- Tu préfères la géographie ou l'histoire?
- Qu'est-ce que tu n'aimes pas?

2 J'aime...

- Madame Massot va poser la question

  'Quelles matières préfères-tu?'
- Ecoute les réponses de David, Myriam, Renaud et Yamina.
- Note les matières qu'ils préfèrent:

  a David   **c** Renaud
  b Myriam   **d** Yamina.

3 Je n'aime pas...

- Madame Massot va poser la question

  'Est-ce qu'il y a des matières que tu n'aimes pas?'
- Ecoute les réponses des élèves.
- Note les matières qu'ils n'aiment pas:

  a David   **c** Renaud
  b Myriam   **d** Yamina.

La Rentrée arrive!

Voici la vitrine d'un magasin...

Le magasin ouvre à quelle heure le 10 septembre et il ferme à quelle heure le 11 septembre?

Dans le cartable...

Voici trois élèves de cinquième. Ils arrivent au collège avec leur cartable...

 1 Ecoutez et regardez

a Voici Myriam...   **b** Voici David...   **c** Voici Yamina...

Elle a...   Il a...   Elle a...

   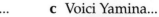

Dans le cartable il y a...   Dans le cartable il y a...   Dans le cartable il y a...

Mots-clés 2

un crayon	pencil
un livre	book
une règle	ruler
un stylo	pen
un cahier	
(de textes)	exercise book
un dictionnaire	dictionary
une trousse	pencil case
une calculatrice	calculator
un cartable	school bag

Tu te rappelles?

avoir	**to have**
j'ai	I have
tu as	you have
il/elle a	he/she has
nous avons	we have
vous avez	you have
ils/elles ont	they have
il y a	there is/there are

 2 Vrai ou faux?

Ecoute bien les dix phrases **a–j**.
Puis, écris V (vrai) ou F (faux).

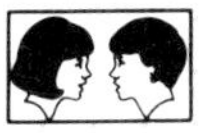

3 **A deux**

a Choisis trois objets que tu as dans ton cartable (en cachette de ton/ta partenaire!).

b Trouve les objets de ton/ta partenaire en posant des questions, par exemple:

'Tu as une trousse dans ton cartable?'

D'abord, décidez qui va commencer!

Casse-tête

Il y a six mots cachés dans la grille.
Voici les définitions:

a Très utile pour les maths!
b ...et très utile pour porter les livres.
c L'histoire, l'anglais, la biologie sont des _____ .
d On écrit avec un _____ .
e On écrit les exercices dans un _____ .
f Fruit

C	B	L	E	M	P	O	M	M	L	I	E
C	A	R	T	A	B	L	E	U	S	O	V
R	I	L	N	F	Y	H	R	S	T	Y	C
A	F	G	C	N	J	Z	Q	M	R	E	A
Y	D	E	Y	U	A	O	U	A	O	H	H
O	R	H	J	P	L	D	A	T	U	C	I
T	I	E	I	Y	B	A	N	I	S	O	E
P	S	V	T	H	D	G	T	E	P	L	R
O	L	S	L	I	X	E	F	R	A	I	O
B	A	N	A	N	R	M	A	E	I	A	T
S	M	X	R	F	C	P	R	S	M	C	R
Q	U	O	R	A	N	G	E	Y	H	A	E

La rentrée des professeurs

Pour les professeurs aussi, c'est la rentrée!

-3 jours

J' ___ les 5ᵉ et les 4ᵉ.

Tu ___ quelles classes cette année?

Madame Félix est professeur d'anglais. La rentrée pour elle, c'est dans trois jours. Elle prépare ses cours dans le jardin.

-1 jour

Oui, mais Rostand ___ content: il n' ___ pas cours le samedi!

Bonjour M. le Directeur.

Le pauvre M. Duval - il ___ les 3ᵉ!

Vous ___ les 4ᵉ cette année, Dusoulier.

Aïe!! J' ___ les troisièmes!!

Chic, je n' ___ pas cours le samedi matin.

C'est la pré-rentrée pour les professeurs. Dans la salle des profs, le directeur distribue les emplois du temps.

-15 min.

Voilà les 6ᵉ - ils ___ petits, n'est-ce pas?

Oui. Regardez le petit Doulon: il ___ très timide!

Mme Félix entre dans la salle des professeurs et dit bonjour à M. Bruno, un prof de maths. Ils regardent les petits sixièmes dans la cour.

-5 min.

good morning My name is M___ ___ lix

22 élèves, c' ___ vraiment bien!

Mme Félix est dans la salle de classe. Elle attend sa classe de cinquième. Elle écrit son nom en anglais sur le tableau.

zéro!

Euh, pardon madame... Vous ___ Mme Félix? Nous ___ les 5ᵉ.

Er, we are the second years.

Oui, je ___ Mme Félix.

But we speak English here. Come in and sit down, please.

Et voici les élèves qui arrivent. L'année scolaire commence!

1   **Trouvez les mots**

In the story, find the French for these words:

a These are all masculine, so need **un** in front of them:
a teacher
a blackboard
a lesson
a timetable.

b These are all feminine, so need **une** in front of them:
a staffroom
a yard/playground
a classroom
a school year.

2   **Avoir et être**

In the speech bubbles, parts of **avoir** (to have) and **être** (to be) have been missed out.

a Write down the correct part of the verb for each space …

b … then explain what all the words in the bubbles mean.

Tu te rappelles?

être	to be
je suis	I am
tu es	you are
il/elle/c'est	he/she/it is
nous sommes	we are
vous êtes	you are
ils/elles sont	they are

3   **Dans**

One French word for 'in' is **dans** (you met it in **Dans le cartable...**). It comes six times in the story: the first is **dans trois jours**, 'in three days'.

a Find the other five **dans** phrases …

b … then say what they mean.

année
19__19__

nom _____
établissement _____
_____
classe _____

CAHIER DE TEXTES

Le cahier de textes

Like most French **collège** pupils, Renaud Feydy
has a **cahier de textes**, in which he notes down
homework (**les devoirs**) and other assignments.

Here are some extracts from his **cahier** …

MATIERES	pour le	TEXTES — LUNDI
Physique	06.10	Contrôle sur toutes les leçons.
Géographie	06.10	aller voir au cinéma une émission sur les incas à 20h 30 (si on peut)

MATIERES	pour le	TEXTES — MARDI
Anglais	16/9	apprendre le vocabulaire
Biologie	16/9	finir le dessin.
Français	07/10	questions n° 4, 5, 3, 7 page 7

MATIERES	pour le	TEXTES — MERCREDI
anglais	10/9	apprendre la grammaire finir l'exercice

MATIERES	pour le	TEXTES — VENDREDI
Musique	10_10	Apprendre " Famille d'instruments "
Math	10_10	Faire signer le contrôle page 26 n°30 ; n° 31 contrôle page

1   Les jours de la semaine

On which day of the week did Renaud get work set for

a   Music?
b   French?
c   Physics?
d   English?

2   Quelle date?

In the **pour le** column, Renaud writes the date when work is due in.
Your teacher will say five dates. Write down one subject he must hand in on each date.

3   Les devoirs

Now look at the work that Renaud has been set.
Some of the words you know already and some you can guess because they are like English words.

What has been set for …

a   French (7 Oct.)?
b   Music (10 Oct.)?
c   English (10 Sept.)?
d   Biology (15 Sept.)?
e   Geography (6 Oct.)?

(If you get stuck, look in the vocabulary at the back of the book, but try to work it out for yourself first!)

Bonnes vacances!

Judging from this poster in a shop window in Caen, some pupils don't have a very restful holiday!

a   Which subjects are offered on the poster?
b   Who are the youngest pupils catered for?
c   What are we told about the size of classes?
d   What do you think this means?

2 heures consécutives par jour et par matière (au choix)

Révisions de Vacances
MATH-PHYSIQUE
ANGLAIS

• de la 6ème à la Terminale.
• Classes de 4 à 6 élèves.
• 2 heures consécutives par jour et par matière (au choix).

"INTER-MATH"
COURS PRIVE
14, rue Michel Servet
14000 CAEN
☎ 31.30.28.01

Unité 2

La vie de tous les jours

When you've finished unit 2 you'll be able to

- say how you start the day
- talk about your pets
- manage a French-style breakfast.

La mère de Caroline n'est pas contente

Caroline Laforgue arrive toujours en retard...

Elle arrive en retard pour le petit déjeuner,

elle arrive en retard au collège,

bref, elle arrive en retard pour tout!

Finalement, sa mère, Madame Laforgue, se décide.

Un jour, sur la porte de sa chambre, Caroline trouve ceci...

21 rue du Muguet

REGLEMENT INTERIEUR

6h 09 se réveiller
6h 10 se lever
6h 15 prendre le petit déjeuner
6h 30 se laver
6h 35 se coiffer
6h 40 s'habiller
7h 00 quitter la maison
7h 50 arriver au collège
16h 45 rentrer
19h 15 dîner
22h 30 se coucher

signé: *Jeanne Laforgue*

mère

1 **Ecoutez**

Caroline regarde la liste...

19

Mots-clés 1

se réveiller	to wake up	**prendre**	to have/take
se lever	to get up	**quitter**	to leave
se laver	to get washed	**rentrer**	to come home
se coiffer	to comb your hair	**dîner**	to have dinner
s'habiller	to get dressed	**le petit déjeuner**	breakfast
se coucher	to go to bed	**en retard**	late

Les verbes réfléchis

Just like **je m'appelle** and **elle s'appelle**, some other verbs need an extra word. They are called reflexive verbs and the first six in *Mots-clés 1* are like this. But they still have just the same endings as all other -ER verbs. For example:

> **se réveiller**
>
> | | |
> |---|---|
> | **je me réveille** | **nous nous réveillons** |
> | **tu te réveilles** | **vous vous réveillez** |
> | **il/elle se réveille** | **ils/elles se réveillent** |

Some parts of **se lever** need an accent as well:

> | | |
> |---|---|
> | **je me lève** | **nous nous levons** |
> | **tu te lèves** | **vous vous levez** |
> | **il/elle se lève** | **ils/elles se lèvent** |

★

2 Ecoutez...puis écrivez...puis parlez: Que fait Caroline?

What does she do at each of the eleven times on her list?
Write your answers in English.

Exemple: 6h 15 - has breakfast

Check your answers with your teacher, then say them in French.

Exemple: 'A 6h 15 elle prend le petit déjeuner.'

3 A deux: Tu te réveilles à quelle heure?

a When do **you** do the eleven things on Caroline's list?
Work out how you would say them in French.

Exemple: 'Je me réveille à sept heures trente.'

All the verbs you need are normal -ER verbs except for **aller** (which you have had already):

> **je vais, tu vas, il/elle va**

and **prendre**:

> **je prends, tu prends, il/elle prend**

b Take it in turns to ask your partner questions.

Exemple: 'Tu te réveilles à quelle heure?'

4 Trouvez les verbes

Unfortunately, this typist doesn't know French and has run all the words together. Can you sort them out? You may need to add an accent or an apostrophe (').

Exemple: tutereveilles *tu te réveilles*

a elleselave
b nousnouscouchons
c ilssereveillent
d tuthabilles
e vousvouscoiffez
f ilseleve
g ellesselavent
h ilarriveenretard
i jevaisaucollege
j elleprendlepetitdejeuner

Le petit déjeuner

En France, au petit déjeuner, on mange souvent du pain avec du beurre et de la confiture.

Ça s'appelle une tartine.

Quelquefois on mange des croissants. (Tu aimes les croissants?)

Souvent, les Français aiment tremper leur tartine ou leur croissant dans leur café (ou café au lait), qu'ils boivent dans un bol ou une grande tasse.

Certains préfèrent le chocolat chaud ou le thé. (Tu préfères le café ou le thé...ou le chocolat chaud?)

De plus en plus de Français prennent des céréales au petit déjeuner, et le visiteur anglais reconnaît dans les supermarchés beaucoup de marques de céréales familières. (Est-ce que tu reconnais ces céréales?)

...et Minette, qu'est-ce qu'elle prend?

Et toi!

- Toi, tu aimes le café?
- Est-ce que tu préfères les céréales ou les tartines?
- Qu'est-ce que tu prends au petit déjeuner?

22

Quelle heure est-il?

1 Regardez et écoutez

il est une heure trente
il est une heure **et demie**

il est **midi**
il est **minuit**

il est dix heures quinze
il est dix heures **et quart**

il est deux heures quarante-cinq
il est **trois** heures **moins le quart**

2 Lisez

So, what must

et quart   et demie   moins le quart   midi   minuit

mean?

3 Maintenant, écoutez et répétez

4 Ecoutez: Quelle heure est-il?

Match up the ten times you hear on the tape with the pictures below.

Exemple: 1 f

a

b
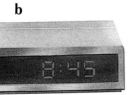

c

VISITES GUIDÉES DE VITRÉ
Vieille ville et château
DÉPART OT-S.I Place S. Yves
10h30   15h   17h

d

SNCF

e

f

g

h

i

RESIDENTS
PARKING PAYANT
De 10h à 12h30
et de 14h30 à 18h

TARIFICATION SPECIFIQUE
8f/24h

APPOSEZ VOTRE MACARON
ET VOTRE TICKET SUR
LE PARE BRISE

j

  5 A deux

a Work out (without your partner seeing) four times using **quart, moins le quart, moins vingt**, etc.

b Draw four blank clock faces.

c Take it in turns to say one of your times to your partner:

Exemple: 'Il est neuf heures moins dix.'

d Your partner fills in this time on a clock face.

Les élèves parlent

 1 Ecoutez

Des élèves du Collège La Guérinière parlent de leur vie de tous les jours.
Ecoute bien, puis réponds aux questions.

a Florent

- What does he do at 7.20?

b Muriel

- What does she do at 6.30 on Monday?
- What does she do next?

c Dorine

- In the evening (**le soir**), what does she do at about 7.15?
- What is the next thing she does?
- What does she do at 10.30?

 2 Renaud

Voici Renaud qui parle. Ecoute bien.
Ecoute encore une fois, puis écris les heures.

Exemple:

a Renaud se lève à 7h 20.

a Renaud se lève à...
b Il prend le petit déjeuner à...
c A..., il se lave et il se coiffe.
d A..., il déjeune.
e Il revient à l'école à...
f Les cours se terminent à...
g Il dîne à...
h Il se couche à...

3 Grégoire

Finalement, c'est Grégoire qui parle.
Ecoute.
Ecoute encore une fois, puis complète:

a Grégoire se l _ _ _ à 7h.
b Il prend son p _ _ _ _ d _ _ _ _ _ _ _ à 7h 30.
c Les cours c _ _ _ _ _ _ _ _ _ à 8h 15.
d A 10h 15 il v _ en récréation.
e A 12h 15 il r _ _ _ _ _ .
f Il d _ _ _ à 19h 30.
g Il va se c _ _ _ _ _ _ à 22h.

Deux verbes

Two of the verbs you have met in this unit work differently from others you have seen.

These are the parts you will need to use:

revenir (to come back) **faire** (to make/do)
je reviens **je fais**
tu reviens **tu fais**
il/elle revient **il/elle fait**

Attention au chien!

je monte la garde

VOUS PÉNÉTREZ
DANS CETTE ENCEINTE A VOS RISQUES ET PÉRILS

a Cet avis (notice) se trouve probablement
  A dans un journal.
  B sur la porte d'un jardin.
  C à l'entrée d'un musée.

b Le chien sur l'avis est
  A un caniche.
  B un setter.
  C un berger allemand.

c 'Je monte la garde' signifie en anglais 'I'm …'

Les animaux

Mots-clés 2

le chat
la chatte

le chien
la chienne

l'oiseau (m)

les oiseaux

le cheval

le lapin

le hamster

les chevaux

la tortue

le poisson rouge

le serpent

le cochon d'Inde

le crocodile

1 **Ecoutez**

2 **Ecoutez: J'ai un animal à la maison**

Huit élèves parlent des animaux qu'ils ont à la maison. Mais...quels animaux ont-ils?

3 Trouvez les animaux

Il y a dix animaux sur l'image...mais ils se cachent!
Regarde bien, trouve les animaux, puis écris leur nom.

Exemple: le chat

His and hers

Ma chatte s'appelle Mizou.

Mon serpent s'appelle Bibi.

Voici mes oiseaux, Hector et Achille.

- **mon**, **ma** and **mes** all mean **my** ...

  So, can you work out when you use which one?
  (Clue: have a good look at the word that comes after.)

- **your** is **ton, ta, tes**

  and

- **his/her** is **son, sa, ses**

  They work in exactly the same way.

Mon, ma, mes

What would be the word for **my** with these words?

a lapin   d crocodiles
b tortue   e chienne
c hamster   f chevaux

2 **Son, sa, ses**

Write down **his** for these words:

a chatte   d oiseau
b serpents   e cochons d'Inde
c tortue   f poisson rouge

Now write down **her** for the same words.

What do you notice about the **his** and **her** lists?

 3 **A deux: Tu as un animal à la maison?**

a Write down a pet you have, or would like to have, at home.

   Exemple: un lapin

   Don't let your partner see!

b Take it in turns to ask questions to find out which pet your partner has.

   Exemple: 'Tu as un cochon d'Inde?'

c Once you have discovered what it is, find out as much as you can
   about it (the person asking the questions will use **ton/ta/tes**, the
   person answering, **mon/ma/mes**).

   Exemples:

   'Ton cochon d'Inde s'appelle...?'
   'Mon cochon d'Inde s'appelle Cachou.'

   'Ta chienne est petite?'
   'Oui, ma chienne est petite.'

d Be prepared to give as complete a description as you can of your
   partner's pet to the rest of the class. Begin with **son/sa/ses**.

   Exemple: 'Son cochon d'Inde s'appelle...'

Dans le journal

ANIMAUX

1 • Vends **5 lapins blancs**, adultes. Tél. 05.00.55.79.

2 • Vds **caniches noir et gris**. Tél. 06.72.75.00.

3 • Vds **couples pigeons**. Tél. 05.90.84.00.

4 • Donne **jolie petite chatte tigrée**. 1 mois. Tél. 04.91.00.77 à partir de 19 h.

5 • Vds **St-Bernard 1 an**, cause déménagement, 600 F. Tél. 05.55.31.37.

6 • Vds **cochon d'Inde**, 15 F pièce. Tél. 05.09.54.47.

7 • Vds **oiseaux exotiques** et **canaris**. Tél. 05.32.45.23 le soir.

8 • Cherche **chiot berger allemand**. Faire offres au 05.84.11.19.

9 • Cause déménagement vends **CHIENNE BERGER ALLEMAND** 1 an, vaccinée, bonne gardienne, bas prix. Tél. 05.31.27.72.

10 • Vends **joli cheval**, 3 ans, à voir. Tél. 05.90.01.63.

1 A vendre

a Which animals feature in each advert?
b What colour are the animals in advert 1?
c … and in 2?
d How old is the animal in 10?
e … and in 4?
f In which advert is an animal being given away?
g … and in which is someone hoping to get one?
h Why is the animal in 5 for sale?
i When should you phone if you want to reply to advert 4?
j … and if you want to answer advert 7?
k Write down as much of the information from advert 9 as you can.

2 Perdu!

These advertisements are about lost animals:

PERDU

• **Perdue** le 26 juin à Chaumont, **petite chatte grise** de 6 mois. Forte récompense. Tél. 05.02.11.27.

• **Egaré** gros chat noir et blanc dans les jardins derrière la Poste. Tél. 05.31.74.10 récompense.

• **IL COURT TOUJOURS!** Ric, petit chien noir–blanc âgé de deux ans et demi. **A L'AIDE!** Tél. 05.32.34.42.

• **S.O.S!** J'ai perdu ma **tortue**, rue Decomble. Récompense. Tél. 05.32.01.45.

• **Perdu** samedi 9.07 berger allemand répondant au nom de Rex. Yeux clairs, oreilles droites. Tél. 05.46.09.94 de 10h à 12h.

Make up your own advertisement for a lost pet (remember, if it is a feminine word like **chatte** or **tortue** you will need to write **perdue**).

Give as many details as you can:

- type of pet
- name
- age
- when lost
- where lost
- reward
- distinguishing marks (e.g. size, colour)
- phone number

Then add a picture of the lost pet.

Unité 3

Ah, la mode!

When you've finished unit 3 you'll

- know the names of lots of clothes
- be able to say what you and other people are wearing
- know how to say something's too big, short, etc.
- be able to buy clothes and shoes in a French shop.

Chic alors!

Quels sont tes vêtements préférés?
Regarde les images et décide!

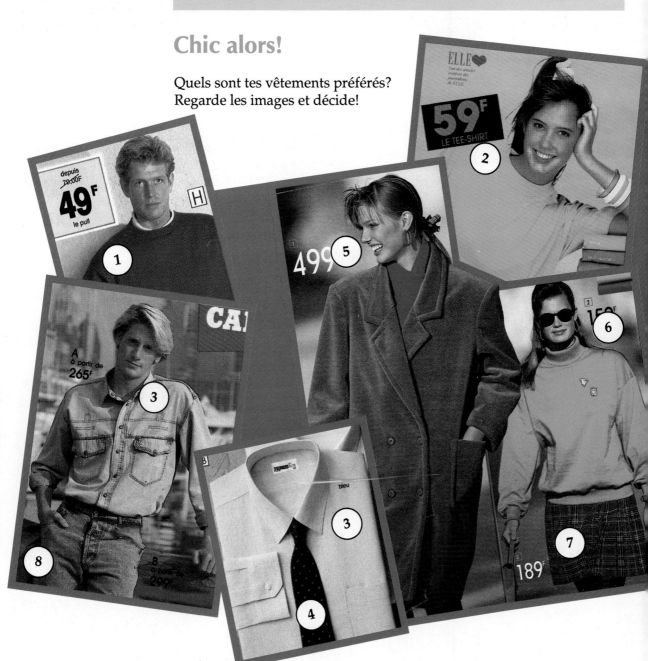

1 un pull-over
2 un tee-shirt
3 une chemise
4 une cravate
5 un manteau
6 un sweat-shirt
7 une jupe
8 un jean
9 un chemisier
10 un blouson
11 un anorak
12 un pantalon
13 une chaussure
14 un jogging
15 une robe
16 un béret
17 un imperméable

La mode écolière

Ecoutez

En France, dans les collèges, les élèves ne portent pas l'uniforme. Ils s'habillent selon leurs préférences.

Regardez la photo.

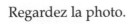

CHAUSSETTES
de Montagne
Adulte

L'uniforme n'existe pas...mais les élèves portent les mêmes sortes de vêtements!

Les filles portent un pull-over ou un sweat-shirt et un pantalon. Les garçons aussi portent un pull ou peut-être une chemise ou un blouson...et bien sûr un pantalon ou un jean.

Spécial montagne

1000 PULLS adulte
Unis ou jacquard
50% laine, 50% acrylique

ANORAK enfant
Avec capuche intérieure
100% poly, 2 tons

BLOUSON enfant
Du 4 au 16 ans, 100% coton
doublure 100% poly

Aux pieds, les élèves portent des chaussures ordinaires ou des chaussures de sport.

C'est le style unisexe!

JEAN Adulte
100% coton indigo
L'inusable

JOGGING
enfant
50% coton 50% acry.

Mots-clés 1

Les vêtements – clothes

Some words for clothes in French are borrowed from English:

un tee-shirt	
un sweat-shirt	
un pull(-over)	
un anorak	

Some are English … but not quite:

un jean	a pair of jeans
un training	a trainer
un jogging	a jogging suit
un costume	a suit

English also borrows from French:

un blouson	
une cagoule	
un béret	

… or sometimes not quite:

une cravate	a tie
une robe	a dress

Here are some more useful words:

une chemise	a shirt
un chemisier	a blouse
une jupe	a skirt
un pantalon	a pair of trousers
un manteau } **un pardessus** }	a (top) coat
un imperméable	a raincoat
une chaussure	a shoe
une chaussette	a sock
une veste } **un veston** }	a jacket
un chapeau	a hat
une sandale	a sandal

Puzzle: Quels vêtements?

Combien de vêtements y a-t-il sur l'image?
Fais une liste des vêtements qui commencent par **c**.

Au collège

1 Yamina et Dorine

Voici Yamina (à droite) qui dit 'bonjour' à sa copine Dorine.
Qu'est-ce que les deux filles portent comme vêtements?

Yamina porte un pull blanc (avec une rayure en couleurs)
un jean
des chaussures de sport noires et blanches
des chaussettes noires.

Et Dorine?
Elle porte   un sweat-shirt vert
un pantalon blanc
des chaussettes blanches
des chaussures jaunes.

2 Christophe et Nicolas

Voici maintenant Christophe (à gauche) qui salue son copain Nicolas.

● Sur un papier, fais deux colonnes.

● Dans la première, fais une liste des vêtements de Christophe...

● Dans la deuxième, fais une liste des vêtements de Nicolas...

Christophe porte	Nicolas porte
un sweat-shirt	une chemise

3 Le pull-over rose

Madame Félix et sa fille Gisèle vont au marché.
Elles cherchent des vêtements pour la Rentrée.

Regarde la photo pendant une minute...puis ferme ton livre.
Décris Gisèle: comment est-elle? (grande/petite? blonde/brune?)
Qu'est-ce qu'elle porte comme vêtements?
Et sa mère?

★ 4 Ecris-moi, s'il te plaît!

Voici une lettre de ton correspondant français:

...Dans mon livre d'anglais
il y a un dessin de deux
élèves anglais qui portent
l'uniforme. ⟶

C'est vraiment comme ça dans
ton collège?
Est-ce que tu portes l'uniforme?
Si oui, comment est-il?
Si non, qu'est-ce que tu portes?

Et qu'est-ce que tu aimes
porter le week-end, si tu
vas à une surprise-partie,
par exemple?

Ecris une réponse à ses questions.

35

A vendre: vêtements et chaussures

These advertisements come from a free newspaper in France:

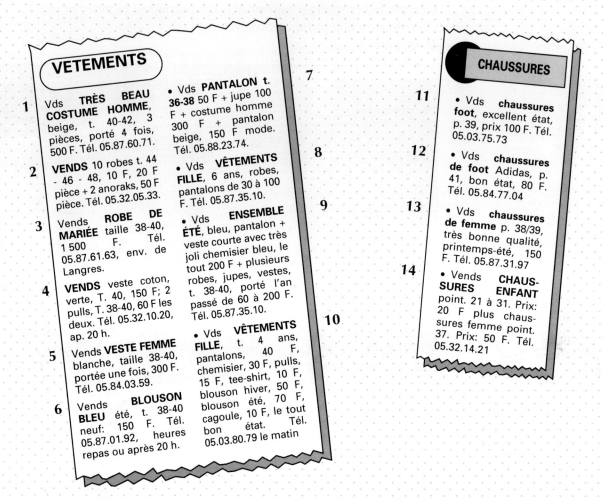

VETEMENTS

1 Vds **TRÈS BEAU COSTUME HOMME**, beige, t. 40-42, 3 pièces, porté 4 fois, 500 F. Tél. 05.87.60.71.

2 **VENDS** 10 robes t. 44 - 46 - 48, 10 F, 20 F pièce + 2 anoraks, 50 F pièce. Tél. 05.32.05.33.

3 Vends **ROBE DE MARIÉE** taille 38-40, 1 500 F. Tél. 05.87.61.63, env. de Langres.

4 **VENDS** veste coton, verte, T. 40, 150 F; 2 pulls, T. 38-40, 60 F les deux. Tél. 05.32.10.20, ap. 20 h.

5 Vends **VESTE FEMME** blanche, taille 38-40, portée une fois, 300 F. Tél. 05.84.03.59.

6 Vends **BLOUSON BLEU** été, t. 38-40 neuf: 150 F. Tél. 05.87.01.92, heures repas ou après 20 h.

• Vds **PANTALON t. 36-38** 50 F + jupe 100 F + costume homme 300 F + pantalon beige, 150 F mode. Tél. 05.88.23.74.

• Vds **VÊTEMENTS FILLE**, 6 ans, robes, pantalons de 30 à 100 F. Tél. 05.87.35.10.

• Vds **ENSEMBLE ÉTÉ**, bleu, pantalon + veste courte avec très joli chemisier bleu, le tout 200 F + plusieurs robes, jupes, vestes, t. 38-40, porté l'an passé de 60 à 200 F. Tél. 05.87.35.10.

• Vds **VÊTEMENTS FILLE**, t. 4 ans, pantalons, 40 F, chemisier, 30 F, pulls, 15 F, tee-shirt, 10 F, blouson hiver, 50 F, blouson été, 70 F, cagoule, 10 F, le tout bon état. Tél. 05.03.80.79 le matin

7

8

9

10

CHAUSSURES

11 • Vds **chaussures foot**, excellent état, p. 39, prix 100 F. Tél. 05.03.75.73

12 • Vds **chaussures de foot** Adidas, p. 41, bon état, 80 F. Tél. 05.84.77.04

13 • Vds **chaussures de femme** p. 38/39, très bonne qualité, printemps-été, 150 F. Tél. 05.87.31.97

14 • Vends **CHAUS-SURES ENFANT** point. 21 à 31. Prix: 20 F plus chaus-sures femme point. 37. Prix: 50 F. Tél. 05.32.14.21

1 Qu'est-ce qu'on vend?

Which items of clothing or footwear are for sale in these advertisements? (If you need help, look again at *Mots-clés 1*.)

a 1
b 5
c 6
d 12
e 13

Some of the advertisements offer more than one type of clothing. Which types of clothes are for sale in these adverts?

f 2
g 4
h 7
i 9
j 10

2 De quelle couleur est...?

Le costume d'homme (annonce 1) est beige.
De quelle couleur est...

a la veste de coton (annonce 4)?
b la veste de femme (annonce 5)?
c le blouson d'été (annonce 6)?
d le pantalon (annonce 7)?
e le chemisier (annonce 9)?

Vital statistics

In the **vêtements** advertisements, you'll have noticed the word **taille** and guessed that it means 'size'.
So in adverts 3 and 5 the size is 38–40 (but beware! these are continental sizes which aren't the same as ours!)

To save space, **t.** is used for **taille**.
In which adverts can you spot it?

For shoes, **pointure** is the word for size. This can be shortened to **point.**, as in advert 14, or just **p.**
In which adverts can you spot it?

Mots-clés 2

Describing clothes

Advert 9 mentions **une veste courte**, a short jacket.
A short jumper would be **un pull court**.
Why is there an **'e'** in the first case but not the second?

Here are some more words you will need to describe clothes:

grand(e)	big
petit(e)	small
serré(e)	tight
large	wide
long(ue)	long

If something is too big, too short, too long, etc., put **trop** in front of the adjective. For example:

trop court

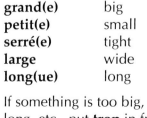

37

Trop...

Why aren't these people happy with their presents?
Say what's wrong, using **trop**.

Exemple:

a 'La jupe de Bernadette est trop courte!'

a Bernadette

b Maurice

c Yvette

d Roland

e Paul

f Lisette

Tailles et pointures

Continental sizes are different from ours, so when you go shopping for clothes or shoes you need to know what size to look or ask for, otherwise you'll probably end up with something far too small!

This table was drawn up to help British tourists by the famous Paris department store *Les Galeries Lafayette*:

The department store, capital of fashion
Le grand magasin, capitale de la mode

Galeries Lafayette
Paris : 40, bd Haussmann et 6 Montparnasse, au pied de la Tour
Nice : place Masséna.

Vêtements/Chaussures: Tailles et pointures

	FEMMES			HOMMES		
	France	Angleterre		France	Angleterre	
Robes,	38	10	Costumes,	38	36	S
manteaux	40	12	vestes	40	37	
	42	14		42	38	
	44	16		44	39	M
	46	18		46	40	L
				48	42	XL
Pull-overs,	38	32	Chemises	36	14	S
chemisiers	40	34		37	$14\frac{1}{2}$	
	42	36		38	15	M
	44	38		39	$15\frac{1}{2}$	
	46	40		40	16	L
	48	42		41	$16\frac{1}{2}$	
Chaussures	35	2	Chaussures	39	$6\frac{1}{2}$	
	$35\frac{1}{2}$	3		40	7	
	36	$3\frac{1}{2}$		41	$7\frac{1}{2}$	
	$36\frac{1}{2}$	4		42	8	
	37	$4\frac{1}{2}$		43	$8\frac{1}{2}$	
	$37\frac{1}{2}$	5		44	9	
	38	$5\frac{1}{2}$		45	10	
	$38\frac{1}{2}$	6				

Mots-clés 3

To ask what size someone takes, say

Quelle taille { **fais-tu?** / **faites-vous?** }   for clothes

or

Quelle pointure { **fais-tu?** / **faites-vous?** }   for shoes

To say what size you take, use   **Je fais du (quarante-deux).**

Quelle taille? Quelle pointure?

- Find out from the list your continental size for
  a blouse or shirt
  a dress or jacket
  trainers.

- Work out how to say the sizes in French (for example,
  46 = **quarante-six**).

- Answer your teacher's questions.

- Using the same questions, take it in turns to ask about your partner's
  sizes.

On achète des vêtements et des chaussures

 1 **Ecoutez**

Listen and find out

- what these people want to buy
- the colour or colours they prefer
- the size they take:

a **Mme Andou**

b **M. Bazile**

c **Nicolas Carron**

d **Mme Delmas**

e **Madeleine Estève**

f **M. Florent**

2 **Super promotion!**

ASSORTIMENT **JUPES FEMME**
Modèles et coloris assortis.
Différentes compositions

La jupe

50F

La 2ème **GRATUITE**

LES 13 - 14 - 15 SEPTEMBR

OPERATION

1 + 1

ACHETE **GRATUIT**

Ce, cette, cet, ces

In the shops you heard assistants say

Ce pantalon noir est très élégant

and **Cette chemise est très belle**.

Ce, **cette** and **cet** all mean 'this' or 'that':

- **Ce** is used with masculine words.

- **Cette** is used with words that are feminine.

- **Cet** is used if the word is masculine and starts with a vowel:

> **cet imperméable** (this/that raincoat)
> **cet anorak** (this/that anorak)

For 'these' or 'those', use **ces**:

> **ces pulls** (these/those pullovers)
> **ces chemises** (these/those shirts)
> **ces imperméables** (these/those raincoats)
> **ces anoraks** (these/those anoraks)

Go through *Mots-clés 1*, putting **ce**, **cette** or **cet** in front of each article of clothing.

3 Quelle fille difficile!

Madame Félix and her daughter (page 35) are still trying to find Gisèle a new outfit for **la Rentrée**. But Gisèle is being more difficult than usual today and doesn't like any of her mother's suggestions.

Note down:

- Madame Félix's five suggestions (**'Tu aimes...?'**)
- Gisèle's own preferences (**'Non, je préfère...'**)

France info: l'année française

Bonne Année

Le jour de l'an: l'année commence.
Le facteur apporte des cartes...
Bonne année!

Valentin Valentine

14 février

POUR UN CADEAU
UNE IDÉE LUMINEUSE
GILLES
DRAPT
Place Diderot - LANGRES
TEL. 25.87.46.91

La Saint-Valentin, c'est
une fête romantique. Les
garçons achètent des
cadeaux pour les filles...
les filles pour les
garçons.

Attention! Voici des poissons d'avril! Au
collège on attache des poissons en papier
dans le dos des camarades.

Joyeuses Pâques

Muguet Porte-Bonheur

Pour Le
1er Mai

RUE
DU MUGUET

Pâques est, avec Noël, la fête
la plus importante de l'année.
Pour les enfants, il y a des
oeufs en chocolat.

Le 1ᵉʳ mai, on offre du muguet
aux amis. C'est une fleur qui
porte bonheur.

42

JUILLET

1 M Thierry
2 J Martinien
3 V Thomas
4 S Florent
5 D Ant.-M.
6 L Mariette
7 M Raoul
8 M Thibaut
9 J Amandine
10 V Ulrich
11 S Benoît
12 D Olivier
13 L Henri/Joël
14 M FÊTE NAT.
15 M Donald
16 J

AOUT

1 S Alphonse
2 D Julien-Ey.
3 L Lydie
4 M JM Vianney
5 M Abel
6 J Transfiguration
7 V Gaétan
8 S Dominique
9 D Amour
10 L Laurent
11 M Claire
12 M Clarisse
13 J Hippolyte
14 V Evrard
15 S ASSOMPTION
16 D Armel
17 L Hyacinthe
18 M Hélène
19 M Jean Eudes
20 J Bernard
21 V Christophe

SEPTEMBRE

11 V Adelphe
12 S Apollinaire
13 D Aimé
14 L Ste-Croix
15 M Roland
16 M Edith
17 J Renaud
18 V Nadège
19 S Émilie
20 D Davy
21 L Matthieu
22 M Maurice
23 M AUT. Q.T.
24 J Thècle
25 V Hermann
26 S Côme/Dam.
27 D Vincent de P.
28 L Venceslas
29 M Michel
30 M Jérôme

OCTOBRE

11 D Firmin
12 L Wilfried
13 M Géraud
14 M Juste
15 J Thér. d'Av
16 V Edwige
17 S Baudouin
18 D Luc
19 L René
20 M Adeline
21 M Céline
22 J Elodie
23 V Jean de Cap.
24 S Florentin
25 D Crénin
26 L Dimitri
27 M Emeline
28 M Simon, Jude
29 J Narcisse
30 V Bienvenue
31 S Quentin

NOVEMBRE

1 D TOUSSAINT
2 L Défunts
3 M Hubert
4 M Charles
5 J Sylvie
6 V Bertille
7 S Carine
8 D Geoffroy
9 L Théodore
10 M Léon
11 M ARMIST. 1918
12 J Christian
13 V Brice
14 S Sidoine
15 D Albert
16 L Marguerite
17 M Elisabeth
18 M Aude
19 J

DECEMBRE

1 M Florence
2 J Viviane
3 V Fr. Xavier
4 S Barbara
5 D Gérald
6 D Nicolas
7 L Ambroise
8 M Imm. Conc.
9 M P. Fourier
10 J Romaric
11 V Daniel
12 S JF de Chant.
13 D Lucie
14 L Odile
15 M Ninon
16 M Alice   Q.T.
17 J Gaël
18 V Gatien
19 S Urbain
20 D Abraham
21 L Pierre C.
22 M HIVER
23 M Armand
24 J Adèle
25 V NOËL
26 S Etienne
27 D JeanA.Sⁿ·F.
28 L Innocents
29 M David
30 M Roger
31 J Sylvestre

Le 14 juillet, c'est la Fête Nationale:
on célèbre la prise de la Bastille,
le 14 juillet, 1789, commencement de
la Révolution française.

Fédération Unie des Auberges de Jeunesse
PRINTEMPTS ETE 92

vacances
activites
programme détaillé

Hourra! Les vacances!

NOËL

CADEAU SURPRISE

Noël...la fête la plus
importante de
l'année. Le père
Noël apporte des
cadeaux pour les
enfants. On mange
une bûche de Noël.
Joyeux Noël!

La Saint-Sylvestre: on dîne au restaurant.

Réveillon

☆

Les cartes

Dessine une carte pour la Saint-Valentin,
pour Pâques ou pour Noël.

Aux magasins

1   A deux: Ah, c'est beau!

Now you know enough to be able to go into a French shop and buy clothes or shoes.
Work with a partner.

a Decide who is the customer (**le client/la cliente**) and who is the shop assistant (**le vendeur/la vendeuse**).

Client(e):
- Choose one item of clothing or footwear from *Mots-clés 1*.
- Work out your size.
- Decide what colour you want.
- Work out how to say you like something.

Vendeur/-euse: Work out how to ask
- what size the customer takes
- what colour he/she prefers
- whether he/she likes something.

b Work this dialogue with your partner.

vendeur/-euse   **client(e)**

- Say hello to the customer

- Say hello back
- Say what item of clothing or footwear you'd like

- Ask what size the customer takes

- Tell him/her

- Ask what colour the customer prefers

- Tell him/her

- Ask if the customer likes this (coat)

- Say yes, it's nice

2 **A deux: C'est pour ma soeur/C'est pour mon frère**

A visitor to Belgium has spotted this souvenir sweatshirt in a shop.
It looks like the ideal present for a sister or brother.
Work out a dialogue with your partner, one being the customer and one the shop assistant.
To help you, look at the dialogue boxes on page 44; what will be different about this conversation?

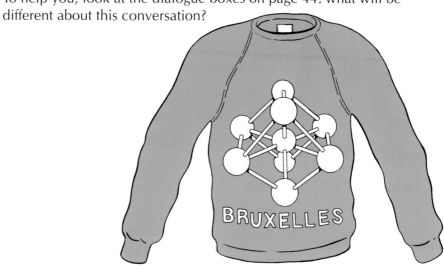

Pour rire

Unité 4

J'ai faim!

When you've finished unit 4 you'll

- know the names of lots of snacks, drinks and ice creams
- be able to buy them at a snack bar, café or stall
- be able to say what people are going to do.

Au Sidney Food...

Le fast-food

En France et en Belgique maintenant il y a beaucoup de restaurants fast-food. On y achète des burgers, des hot-dogs, des sandwichs, etc.

Mais attention! Ces mots anglais et américains se prononcent à la française!

1   Ecoutez

Regarde les quatre listes et écoute Nicolas...

Mots-clés 1

un croissant	croissant	**une quiche**	quiche
un (ham)burger	(ham)burger	**une pizza**	pizza
un hot-dog	hot dog	**une grillade**	grill
un sandwich	sandwich	**une salade composée**	
un plat chaud	hot meal to take away	**une salade mixte**	mixed salad
j'ai faim	I'm hungry	**une tartelette**	small tart
		une boisson	drink
		une glace	ice cream

2 Je vais...

Tu as faim et tu aimes les pizzas.
Alors tu vas au Sidney Food ou au Mandarin.
Où vas-tu pour acheter...

a un croissant?
b une quiche?
c une glace?
d un sandwich?

e un hot-dog?
f une tartelette?
g une salade composée?
h un burger?

3   A deux: Où vas-tu?

Partenaire A pose les questions.
Partenaire B choisit le restaurant et le fast-food.
A la fin de chaque conversation, changez de rôle.

Au snack-bar

Ecoutez

Tu as faim.
Tu voudrais un sandwich.
Tu arrives dans un snack-bar.
Qu'est-ce que tu demandes?
Ecoute ce client qui choisit un sandwich...

Mots-clés 2

To ask what kind of sandwiches they have in a snack-bar, say	**Qu'est-ce que vous avez comme sandwichs?**
To ask if they have any sandwiches, say	**Vous avez des sandwichs?**
Here's a selection you might be offered:	**un sandwich au jambon** ham
	au pâté pâté
	au fromage cheese
	au saucisson slicing sausage

A Riva Bella

Les personnes sur la photo sont en vacances à Riva Bella, près de Caen.

Il est midi et ils ont faim.
Qu'est-ce qu'ils vont acheter au snack-bar?

1 Lisez et parlez

Imagine you're there too, with some friends who don't speak French.

a Tell them four different kinds of things they can eat here.

b Now look at the sandwich list.
Explain as best you can the different kinds of sandwiches on offer.

★ **2 Ecrivez**

Decide what you'd like to buy.
Then write down how you think the conversation between you and the shopkeeper will go.

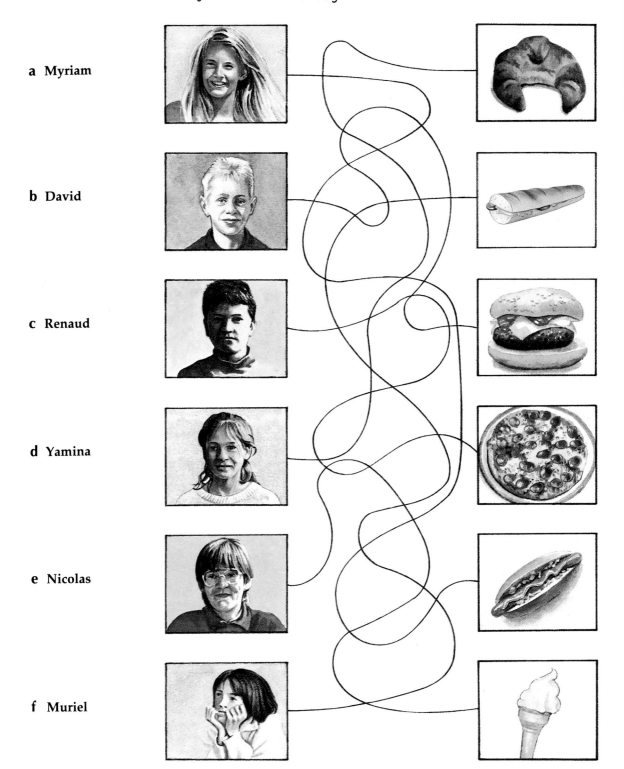

UNITE 4

3 Qu'est-ce qu'ils choisissent?

Un groupe de camarades mangent dans un restaurant fast-food.
Ils regardent le menu...
Qu'est-ce qu'ils choisissent?

Exemple:

a Myriam choisit un hot-dog.

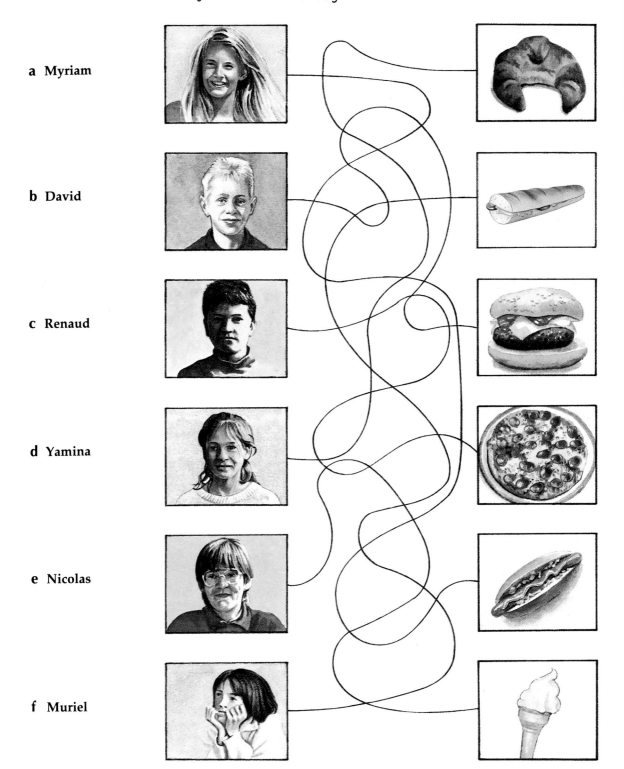

a Myriam

b David

c Renaud

d Yamina

e Nicolas

f Muriel

51

★ 4 **C'est compliqué!**

Choisis un mot simple (par exemple: **une quiche**) pour remplacer les longues définitions de ces clients du restaurant fast-food:

Je prends une tarte italienne à base de pâte à pain garnie de tomates, anchois, olives, etc.

a

Moi, je préfère une saucisse de Francfort servie chaude dans un petit pain.

b

J'ai faim! J'achète une sorte de tarte garnie d'une préparation à base de crème et d'oeufs, et contenant des petits morceaux de lard et de jambon.

c

Je choisis un bifteck haché rond, servi dans un pain rond.

d

Je n'ai pas faim. J'achète une petite pâtisserie feuilletée, salée, en forme de croissant.

Je prends un mets constitué de deux tranches de pain entre lesquelles on place des aliments froids (jambon, viande, saucisson, fromage, salade, etc.).

e

f

LE RAPIDILLY

a
b
c
d
e
f
g
h

J'achète une petite tarte individuelle.

Pour moi, c'est un entremets chaud fait de pain de mie grillé avec du jambon et du fromage.

g

h

-IR verbs

You're already familiar with the -ER family of verbs (**aimer**, **habiter**, etc.). Now it's time to meet a different group: -IR verbs.

You've met parts of one already: **il/elle choisit** and **ils choisissent**, from **choisir**, to choose. The complete verb looks like this:

je choisis	I choose	**nous choisissons**	we choose
tu choisis	you choose	**vous choisissez**	you choose
il/elle choisit	he/she chooses	**ils/elles choisissent**	they choose

This advertisement says 'When you know what it costs you choose Mammouth!'

maison-jardin

QUAND ON SAIT CE QUE ÇA COÛTE
ON CHOISIT MAMMOUTH !

mammouth

-IR verbs are a small group.
The only other really common one is **finir**, to finish:
can you work out what the whole verb looks like?

Choisir...ou finir?

A part of **choisir** or **finir** has been left out of these sentences.

- What should go in each space?

- What does the complete sentence mean?

a Qu'est-ce qu'elle _____ comme sandwich?
b Moi, je _____ une pizza.
c Nicolas _____ son petit déjeuner.
d Je _____ mon exercice de maths.
e Alors, tu _____ ce pantalon rouge?
f Au collège les cours _____ à cinq heures.

TARIF NET
POUR TOUT LITIGE
S'ADRESSER A LA CAISSE SVP

PANACHE PEPSI COLA LIMONADE	12 00
DIABOLO MENTHE OU FRAISE	12 00
BIERE -CELTA-	10
SIROP A L'EAU	12 00
CHOCOLAT CHAUD OU FROID	12 00
THE NATURE	12 00
THE AU LAIT OU CITRON	15 00
THE FROID CITRON	15 00
CAFE FROID	
GRAND CAFE 10 EXPRESS 8 00	
EXPRESS AVEC POT DU LAIT OU VERRE EVIAN	10 00
CAPOUCCINO KAFFEE MIT SAHNE	17 00
INFUSION	12 00
CAFE CREME AVEC CHANTILLY	17 00
CAFE AU LAIT	12 00
EAU MINERALE VICHY VITTEL PERRIER	12 00
AVEC SIROP OU TRANCHE CITRON	12 00
GINY SCHWEPPES ORANGINA	15 00
RICQLES	15 00
JUS DE FRUIT	15 00
CITRON PRESSE	15 00
ORANGE PRESSEE	12 00
LAIT CHAUD	10
LAIT FROID	12 00
LAIT PARFUME FRAISE	12 00
OU MENTHE	15 00
BITTER SANPELLEGRINO	
MILK-SHAKE	20 00
VANILLE CHOCOLAT FRAISE	0
OU BANANE	
	2

EN COMPLEMENT PETIT VERRE 'EVIAN'
TOUT SUPPLEMENT SIROP CITRON LAIT

**CONSOMMATIONS OBLIGATOIRES
POUR TOUTES PERSONNES ASSISES**

La Coupole
**BAR
BRASSERIE
RESTAURANT
AU 1ER ETAGE
*
OUVERT LE
DIMANCHE**

J'ai soif!

This is the kind of price list you will see outside a café in French-speaking countries.

- Which drinks can you identify?

1 Ecoutez

When you've chosen what you'd like, how do you go about ordering?
Listen to this group discussing what to have, then speaking to the waiter.

- What three drinks did they choose?

2 Ecoutez

It's usual to pay for your drinks at the end, just before you leave. Listen to the same people paying for what they've had.

- How much did the drinks come to?

- Did they have to leave a tip?

Mots-clés 3

une limonade	lemonade	j'ai soif	I'm thirsty
une bière	beer	c'est combien?	how much is it?
(for draught beer, ask for **un demi pression**)		s'il vous plaît!	please! (to call the waiter)
un panaché	shandy		
un chocolat chaud/froid	hot/cold drinking chocolate	le service est compris?	is service included?
un thé (au lait/ au citron)	tea (with milk/ lemon)	qu'est-ce que tu prends?	what are you having?
un café/ un express	black coffee	un garçon un serveur	waiter
un café crème/ au lait	white coffee	une serveuse	waitress
un Orangina	fizzy orange drink		
un lait	milk		

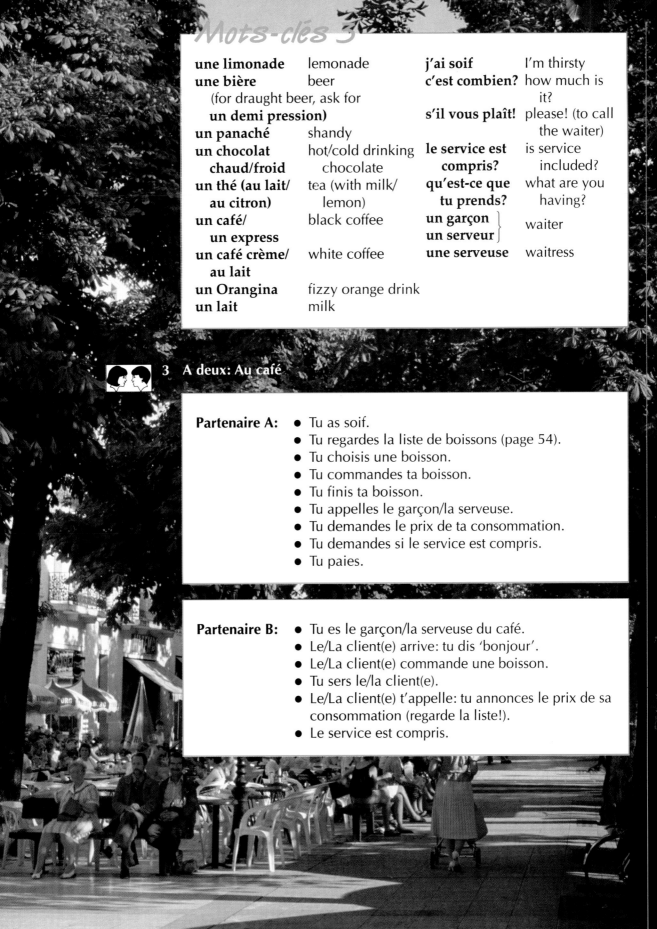

3 A deux: Au café

Partenaire A:
- Tu as soif.
- Tu regardes la liste de boissons (page 54).
- Tu choisis une boisson.
- Tu commandes ta boisson.
- Tu finis ta boisson.
- Tu appelles le garçon/la serveuse.
- Tu demandes le prix de ta consommation.
- Tu demandes si le service est compris.
- Tu paies.

Partenaire B:
- Tu es le garçon/la serveuse du café.
- Le/La client(e) arrive: tu dis 'bonjour'.
- Le/La client(e) commande une boisson.
- Tu sers le/la client(e).
- Le/La client(e) t'appelle: tu annonces le prix de sa consommation (regarde la liste!).
- Le service est compris.

J'aime les glaces!

1 Quel parfum?

Tu aimes les glaces?
Oui, bien sûr!
En France il y a un grand choix de parfums: regarde la liste...

- Quel est ton parfum préféré?

- Est-ce qu'il y a un parfum que tu n'aimes pas?

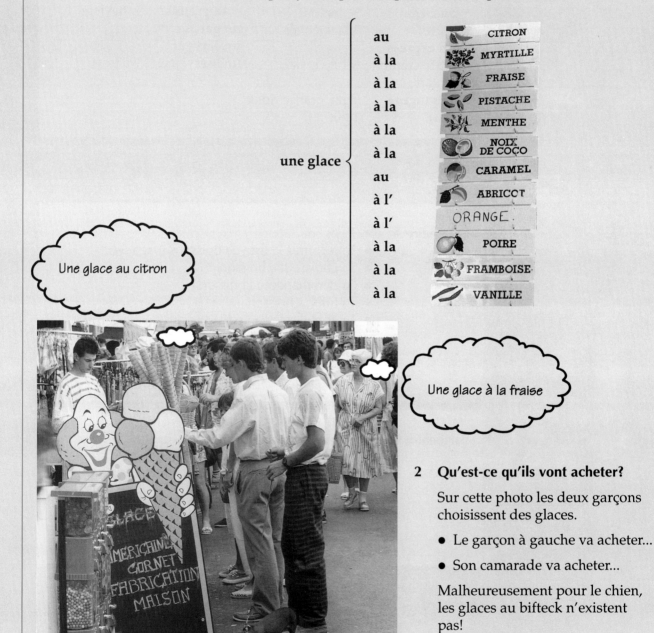

	au	CITRON
	à la	MYRTILLE
	à la	FRAISE
	à la	PISTACHE
	à la	MENTHE
une glace	à la	NOIX DE COCO
	au	CARAMEL
	à l'	ABRICOT
	à l'	ORANGE
	à la	POIRE
	à la	FRAMBOISE
	à la	VANILLE

Une glace au citron

Une glace à la fraise

2 Qu'est-ce qu'ils vont acheter?

Sur cette photo les deux garçons choisissent des glaces.

- Le garçon à gauche va acheter...

- Son camarade va acheter...

Malheureusement pour le chien, les glaces au bifteck n'existent pas!

Sur la liste, il y a 'glaces au bifteck'?

3 A deux

Avec ton/ta partenaire, imagine une petite conversation entre le garçon qui achète une glace au citron et le serveur.

Mots-clés 4

To say you're going to buy
something, use **Je vais acheter...**

To say you're going to
choose something, use **Je vais choisir...**

un parfum flavour
quel parfum? what flavour?

Tu te rappelles?

aller to go

je vais
tu vas
il/elle va
nous allons
vous allez
ils/elles vont

4 Qu'est-ce qu'ils vont faire?

● Regarde bien les dix images.

● Choisis le bon verbe dans le sac.

● Fais une phrase pour les dix personnes.

Exemple: **a** Anne-Claire va acheter une glace.

a Anne-Claire

b Benoît

c Cécile

habiter

porter manger

avoir

regarder

acheter prendre

d David

e Eric

f Frédéric

g Ghislain

écouter se lever

h Hélène

choisir

i Isabelle

j Jérôme

France info: Météo

When you go to France on holiday, with friends or with your family, it could be very useful to work out what the weather has in store for you. And if **you** are seen as the French expert, it might be just as well to get it right …

Prévisions pour aujourd'hui

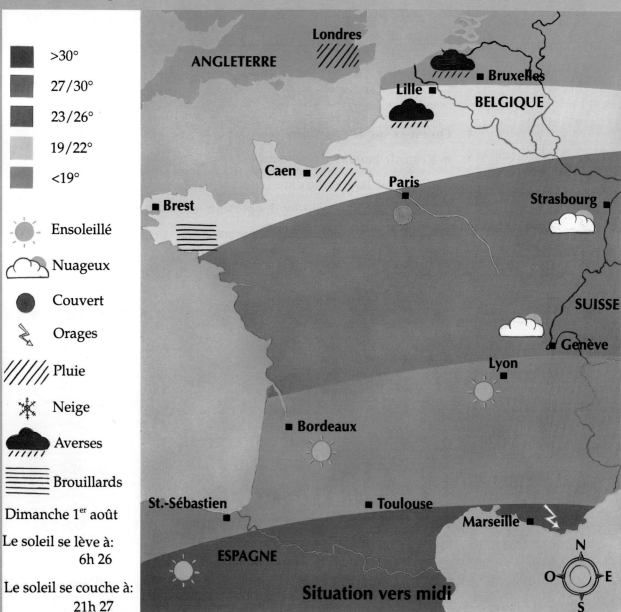

>30°
27/30°
23/26°
19/22°
<19°

Ensoleillé
Nuageux
Couvert
Orages
Pluie
Neige
Averses
Brouillards

Dimanche 1er août

Le soleil se lève à:
6h 26

Le soleil se couche à:
21h 27

Situation vers midi

Look at the weather map and see how much you can work out:

a What day and date is this forecast for?
b Look at the symbols and decide what each one means.
c What is the temperature band for
  - Lyon?
  - Paris?
  - Marseille?
d Which French word on the map means
  - England?
  - Spain?
  - Switzerland?
e What time will sunset be?
f The map shows the situation at what time of day?
g Can you remember which French word 'N' on the compass stands for?
h ... and what about 'O'?
i Imagine you're starting a holiday. You're on the ferry and will be arriving near Caen in about three hours' time. What do you expect the weather to be like?
j Later in the week you'll be going on to Bordeaux. If the weather stays the same, what can you expect?

Quel temps fait-il?

Sur la carte météorologique...		Quand on parle...
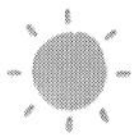 ☀	Ensoleillé	il fait du soleil il fait beau
 ☁	Nuageux	le temps est nuageux
●	Couvert	le ciel est couvert
 ⚡	Orages	il y a des orages
 /////	Pluie	il pleut
 ❄	Neige	il neige
 ☁///	Averses	il y a des averses
 ≡	Brouillards	il y a du brouillard

59

Unité 5

Reprise 1

How much can you remember? In this section you will have another chance to practise the things you learnt in units 1 to 4 ... and to show how much you know!

Au pressing

Look at this price list in a dry cleaner's ...

a What can you have cleaned most cheaply of all?

b Which two garments are the same price if you have them cleaned at the 'economy' rate?

c For one item, there is an 8F price difference between the 'top quality' and the 'economy' rates. Which is it?

d What can you have cleaned at the 'top quality' rate for 28F?

e What is the most expensive item on the list?

f Which is the only item of clothing you haven't been asked to identify?

On va manger!

You're on the beach at Riva Bella. It's midday and you're ready for a snack …

1 Lisez

What foods can you identify on the sign on the corner in front of the shop? (**Un beignet** is a kind of doughnut, **les chips** aren't chips!)

2 Parlez

How would you ask the shopkeeper

- if he has any hot dogs?
- what sort of sandwiches he has?
- how much the **beignets** are?
- for a strawberry ice cream?

3 A deux

Imaginez une conversation entre • le/la touriste
et • le vendeur/la vendeuse.

Pour rire

C'est fatigant,
le fast-food!

Les glaces Gervais

France, Belgium and Switzerland have their own favourite brands of ice cream. **Gervais** is a large firm that sells all sorts of dairy products as well as ice cream; look out for them in your local supermarket.

1 Répondez

a C'est combien, un *Crokim*?
b ...un *Trialo*?
c ...et un *cornet Gervais*?
d Si tu as 3F 50, tu choisis quelle glace?
e Regarde les *Crok'Fruit*. Quels parfums y a-t-il?
f ...et quels parfums y a-t-il pour les *Kimy*?
g Si tu aimes la noix de coco, tu choisis quelle glace?

2 Ecoutez

- Robert et son ami Nicolas choisissent des glaces: quelles glaces?

- Robert achète les glaces à la serveuse: quel parfum demande-t-il?

- Il demande le prix: c'est combien?

- Mais...est-ce qu'il y a une erreur?

3 A deux

Partenaire A: Tu achètes une glace (attention au prix!).
Partenaire B: Tu es le serveur/la serveuse.

Imaginez une conversation entre les deux.

Identités

Voici quatre filles. Elles s'appellent Marianne, Sabine, Nathalie et Irène.

Il y a aussi quatre garçons. Ils se nomment Matthieu, Fabrice, Denis et Edouard.

Mais...c'est à toi de trouver l'identité de chacun.

a Ecris une liste des prénoms (Marianne
Sabine
etc.)

b Ecoute bien et regarde les vêtements des huit personnes.

c Choisis le numéro (1, 2, etc.) qui correspond à chaque prénom.

TARIF NET

IN CASE OF COMPLAINTS
PLEASE GO TO THE CASH DESK

PAIN GRILLE BEURRE CONFITURE	18
CROISSANT	5
SALADE OEUF TOMATES SALADE	30
OMELETTE NATURE	30
JAMBON OU FROMAGE	36
AU FINES HERBES	36
CROQUE MONSIEUR	20
PIZZA	30
QUICHE LORRAINE	30
HAMBURGER	25
OEUF AU PLAT NATURE	25
AVEC JAMBON	36
LASAGNES	40
ASSIETTE DE CHARCUTERIE	40
ASSIETTE DE FRITES	
STEAK HACHE FRITES	
SANDWICHS JAMBON OU SAUCISSON OU FROMAGE	15
PAIN-SALADE SALADE TOMATES OEUF	20
TARTE	20
TARTE MIT SAHNE	30
TOUT SUPPLEMENT PAIN KETCHUP BEURRE MOUTARDE	2
SOUPE	22
PORTION DE FROMAGE	22
POULET FROID OU CHAUD	
COTE DE PORC	
½ COQUELET	
ENTRECOTE	
CHAQUE VIANDE OU VOLAILLE EST ACCOMPAGNE DE SALADE	
BOITE DE COCA-COLA 33 cl.	15
BOITE DE ORANGINA 33 cl	15
RAISONABLE COCKTAIL TROPICAL 50 cl.	30

THESE SEATS ARE RESERVED FOR CLIENTELLE ONLY

a How much would you have to pay for a **croissant** here?

b How much is a hamburger?

c What is the first item on the menu?

d What three kinds of sandwiches are available?

e What would you expect to get if you ordered **une assiette de frites**?

f No price is given for this item. How would you ask the waiter how much **frites** are?

g Can you remember what **une côte de porc** is?

h You have to pay a 2 franc supplement if you have bread, ketchup, butter or … what do you think **moutarde** is?

i Item 3 (**SALADE oeuf, tomates, salade**) might appear on another menu as **salade** _____ .

j Coca-Cola and Orangina come in **boîtes**. What do you think **une boîte** is, in this case?

k Words from how many different languages can you spot on the menu?

Hourra! Les vacances!

Ta correspondante française est en vacances en Bretagne. Elle t'envoie cette carte...

1 Lisez

What is the message?

2 Répondez

    a Quel temps fait-il?
    b Imagine...qui sont les trois personnes?
    c Décris le monsieur...
    d ...et le garçon.

★ **3 Imaginez**

Qu'est-ce qu'ils disent?

Qu'est-ce qu'ils vont faire?

Imaginez

Exemple:

a Amadou va choisir un tee-shirt.
(Amadou's going to choose a tee-shirt.)

a Amadou

b Renaud

c Yamina

d Carole   Gaëlle

e Grégoire

13 ANS
Bon Anniversaire

GOOD MORNING!

HELLO!

f Muriel

g Nicolas   David

h Myriam

i toi!

Applaudissez!

Here are some more -IR verbs you may come across (see page 53). What do they mean?

This television producer is asking her audience to _____ .

This post office advertisement is telling people not to forget to _____ their letters.

This roadside poster is asking motorists to _____ because there may be children about.

Interview avec Alain

Ecoutez

Voici les questions de l'interviewer.
Ecoute bien et note les réponses d'Alain.

Interviewer: Tu rentres du collège à quelle heure?
Alain:

    I: Quand tu arrives, qu'est-ce que tu fais?
    I: Tu prends quoi?
    I: Et tu bois...?
    I: Et après, qu'est-ce que tu fais?
    I: Jusqu'à quelle heure?
    I: Alors, en général?
    I: Et qu'est-ce que tu fais après?
    I: Tu dînes à quelle heure?
    I: Et qu'est-ce que tu prends?
    I: Et après le dîner...?
    I: A quelle heure tu te couches, généralement?

Bonne Rentrée!

VACANCES SCOLAIRES

Toussaint: du mardi 24 octobre après la classe au lundi 6 novembre au matin
Noël: du vendredi 22 décembre après la classe au jeudi 4 janvier au matin
Hiver: du mardi 6 février après la classe au lundi 19 février au matin
Printemps: du mardi 3 avril après la classe au mardi 17 avril au matin
Eté: samedi 30 juin après la classe.

TRANSPORT DES ELEVES
LES REGLES DU JEU
1
Je ne joue pas sur la chaussée.
2
Le car arrive: je me recule et attends l'arrêt complet avant de monter.
3
Je reste assis dans le car.
4
Je range mon sac sous les sièges.
5
J'attends l'arrêt complet avant de me lever.
6
Quand je suis descendu, je laisse s'éloigner le car, je regarde à droite et à gauche avant de traverser.

La journée d'une serveuse de café

Voici Florence.

Elle travaille au Café des Sports.
Elle parle maintenant de sa journée...
qui commence à six heures du matin!

Ecoutez

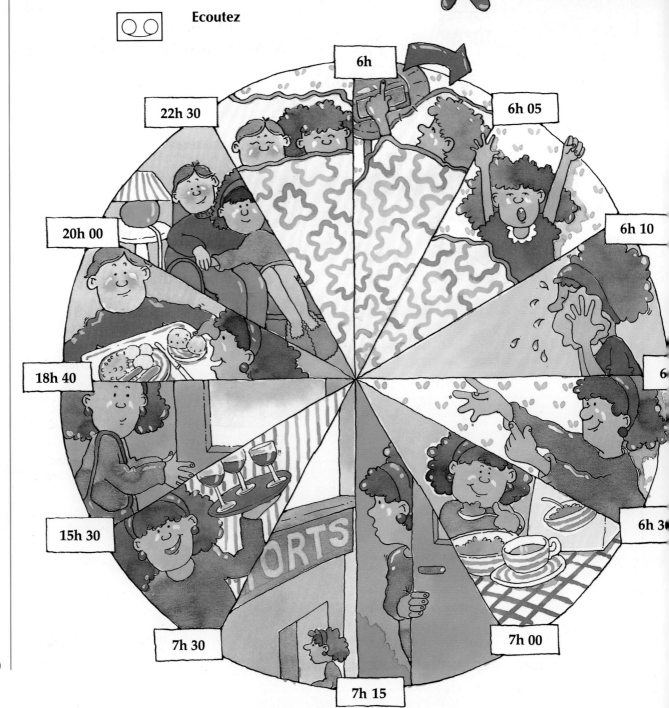

A la terrasse d'un café

Voici trois jeunes gens assis à la terrasse d'un café près d'un lac. Ils sont en vacances...

1   As-tu bonne mémoire?

- Regarde la scène pendant 60 secondes.
- Ferme le livre.
- Ecris cinq phrases sur cette scène.

2   Ecrivez ★

Ecris une description de la scène.

3   A quatre

Les rôles:
   trois clients
   le garçon/la serveuse

- Les clients choisissent un fast-food, une boisson ou une glace...
- Le garçon/La serveuse prend leur commande...

Imaginez la conversation entre les quatre.

C'est horrible!

These awful restaurant jokes come from Belgian local newspapers, but they may be familiar. Can you work out an English version of each one?

a

— Garçon! Il y a une mouche dans ma soupe!
— C'est vrai, monsieur. C'est la spécialité du chef.

b

— Garçon! Vous servez des crabes?
— Asseyez-vous, monsieur. Ici, nous servons n'importe qui.

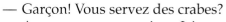

c

— Garçon! Vous avez des pieds de porc?
— Non, monsieur. Je marche toujours comme ça.

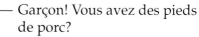

JEUX

Au marché aux animaux

Chacun des enfants va choisir un des six animaux. Mais...quel animal est-ce que chacun des six va acheter? C'est à toi de trouver.

> J'aime bien les chats, mais je préfère les oiseaux.

> Je n'aime pas les oiseaux, mais j'adore les chats.

Laurent

Agnès

> Je ne suis pas attiré par les cochons d'Inde, mais j'aime beaucoup les poissons rouges.

Martin

André

> Je ne suis pas attirée par les tortues, mais j'aime les serpents.

> Mm...je déteste les chats et les tortues et je n'aime pas tellement les serpents.

> Je n'aime pas tellement les poissons, mais j'aime moins les serpents. Les tortues, ça va!

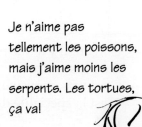

Sênami

Olivier

72

JEUX

Le vêtement caché

Pour trouver le vêtement caché, écris les initiales des illustrations dans les cases correspondantes.

JEUX

Les chaussettes mélangées

- Combien de paires de chaussettes trouves-tu?
- Quelles chaussettes forment une paire? (Donne un numéro et une lettre.)
- De quelle couleur sont-elles?
- Quelle paire préfères-tu?

Combien de touristes?

Un groupe de touristes s'installe à la terrasse d'un café.
Le garçon arrive. Il prend leur commande.
Il apporte   de la bière.
           du vin
           du café.

● Chaque touriste prend une boisson, sauf (except) un, qui n'a pas soif.

● Tous les touristes sauf trois prennent une bière.

● Tous les touristes sauf trois prennent un vin.

● Tous les touristes sauf trois prennent un café.

QUESTION: Combien de touristes y a-t-il dans le groupe?

Le plat caché

Ecris dans la grille les fast-food représentés par les images.
Tu vas trouver dans une colonne verticale un plat caché.
Qu'est-ce que c'est?

Au café

Cette cliente aime beaucoup les puzzles!
Qu'est-ce qu'elle commande au garçon?

Tu commences par ⎡U⎤ et tu vas horizontalement ou verticalement
dans les deux sens (⇄ ou ↑↓).

E	A	U	N	D	A	U
H	T	L	A	W	H	P
U	N	A	S	I	C	A
!	T	I	N	U	E	T
A	I	T	E	T	S'	I
L	P	S	U	O	V	L

Calculez!

Grégoire et Renaud ont chacun plusieurs lapins.

Si Grégoire donne un de ses lapins à Renaud,
ils vont avoir, tous les deux, le même nombre.

Mais si Renaud donne un de ses lapins à
Grégoire, Grégoire va avoir le double.

Combien de lapins ont-ils?

Fais des mots

Forme quatre groupes de trois mots qui commencent par les mêmes lettres.

Exemple:
F R ──── ERE
    ──── OID
    ──── OMAGE

a
── MBE
── RDIN
── MBON

b
── TEAU
── RE
── UCHE

c
── SON
── NTENANT
── S

d
── PEAU
── T
── MBRE

Définitions

1 **a** Le contraire de 'noir'

a | | | A | | |

b Le contraire de 'froid'

b | | | A | | |

c Le contraire de 'petit'

c | | | A | | |

d Le contraire de 'après'

d | | | A | | |

2 **a** Fruit

a | | | I | | |

b Petit chien

b | | | I | | |

c Moyen de transport

c | | | I | | |

d Six _____ deux font quatre

d | | | I | | |

e En hiver, il _____

e | | | I | | |

77

Unité 6

Dieppe, me voici!

As well as being a good place to stay, Dieppe is one of Britain's gateways to Europe.

When you've finished unit 6 you'll be able to

- find out what there is to do in the town
- find your way about
- say what you can do …
- … and understand notices saying what you **can't** do
- buy stamps and write a postcard
- cope with numbers in the hundreds and thousands.

DIEPPE

Londres

Newhaven

Boulogne

Ile de Wight

Durée de la traversée: 4h

LA MANCHE

Cherbourg

Dieppe

SEINE MARITIME (76)

Caen

Rouen

CALVADOS (14)

Paris

Tu vas à Dieppe? Alors, pas de problème! Tu vas à Newhaven, tu prends le bateau, tu traverses la Manche …et tu arrives à Dieppe!

Une fois à Dieppe, tu cherches un plan de la ville.

Qu'est-ce qu'il y a à faire…à voir? Il y a un Office de Tourisme?
Bien sûr, le voilà…

Alors, tu vas à l'Office de Tourisme demander des renseignements…

Office de Tourisme

A l'Office de Tourisme

1 Ecoutez et regardez

a Le port

b Le château

c Le marché

d Le marché aux poissons

e Le parc

f La plage

g La Grande Rue

2 Orientations

A l'Office de Tourisme il y a cinq touristes anglais qui demandent des renseignements à l'employée.
Voici les réponses de l'employée...

1 Le parc Jehan Ango? Alors, c'est tout près. Tournez à droite, et le parc est à droite.

2 Le château? Ah! c'est assez loin. Tournez à gauche, suivez le boulevard du Général de Gaulle et continuez tout droit. Puis, il y a une petite rue qui monte au château.

3 Le marché aux poissons... Tournez à droite, puis au bout du boulevard du Général de Gaulle, tournez à gauche. Le marché aux poissons est juste après le quai Duquesne. C'est tout près de la Gare Maritime.

4 La Grande Rue? Alors, tournez à gauche, suivez le boulevard du Général de Gaulle et prenez la troisième rue à droite. C'est la rue Victor Hugo, je crois. Au fond, à droite, il y a la Grande Rue. C'est près de la rue Saint-Jacques.

5 Pour aller au marché, alors, tournez à gauche et prenez la première à droite. Continuez tout droit, traversez la rue d'Ecosse puis, dans la rue Saint-Jacques, tournez à droite. Le marché est entre l'église et la Place Nationale.

a Quelle est la destination de chaque touriste...en anglais?

Mots-clés 1

(tout) près (de)	(very) near (to)	**monter**	to go up
(assez) loin	(quite) far	**suivez**	follow
après	after	**la gare**	station
entre	between	**l'église (f)**	church
au bout de	at the end of	**la mer**	sea
traverser	to cross		

b Maintenant, regarde le plan de la ville.
Quelle lettre correspond à la destination de chacun des cinq touristes?
Ecris le numéro (1–5) et la lettre correspondante (A–E).

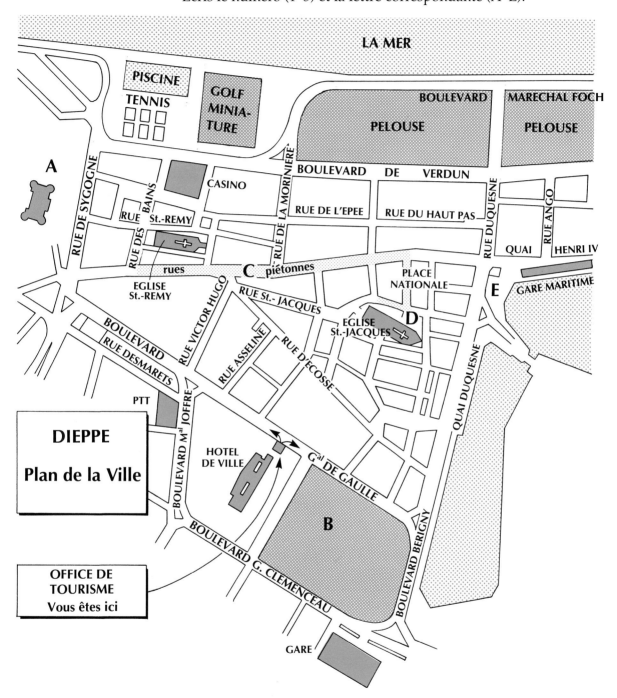

c Two of the English tourists (2 and 5) are having difficulty in understanding the directions. Explain to them what the lady in the tourist office said.

 d Prépare des renseignements pour aider un touriste qui va

- à la gare
- à la Poste (PTT)
- au casino
- à l'Hôtel de Ville
- à la mer
- à l'église St.-Rémy.

Bonjour...de Dieppe!

Voici un timbre-poste français.

On achète les timbres à la poste (ou PTT, voir la page 94) ou dans un bureau de tabac.

Tu peux aussi acheter des cartes postales dans beaucoup de bureaux de tabac.

Voici des touristes qui choisissent des cartes à Dieppe. L'homme à gauche, qui porte le tee-shirt rouge, est suisse. Il choisit sa carte et va à la caisse.

 1 Ecoutez la conversation

Mots-clés 2

un timbre(-poste)	(postage) stamp
un timbre à 2F 20	a 2F 20 stamp
C'est combien, un timbre pour (la Suisse)?	
How much is a stamp for (Switzerland)?	
un bureau de tabac	tobacconist's
une caisse	cash desk
une carte postale	postcard

 2 A deux: Au bureau de tabac

Ecoute encore une fois la conversation entre le touriste suisse et la caissière, puis

● pratique la conversation avec ta/ton partenaire

ou

 ● prépare une autre conversation pour la jeune fille sur la photo. Elle est hollandaise: elle habite la Hollande.

3 Je suis en Italie!

Voici une carte de ta copine suisse, Line:

Bonjour !
Me voici à San Marino, en
Italie ! Je m'amuse beaucoup
et il fait très beau.
Ecris bientôt,
Amitiés,
          Line

A Dieppe, tu achètes cette carte pour Line.

Mots-clés 3

There are various ways of signing off:

Amitiés	Best wishes, regards
Au revoir	Goodbye
A bientôt ⎫ **A samedi** ⎭	See you soon/on Saturday
Ton ami(e)	Your friend
Cordialement	All the best
Ecris bientôt	Write soon

Maintenant, écris la carte à Line.

Bienvenue à Dieppe!

A l'Office de Tourisme tu trouves des renseignements sur Dieppe...

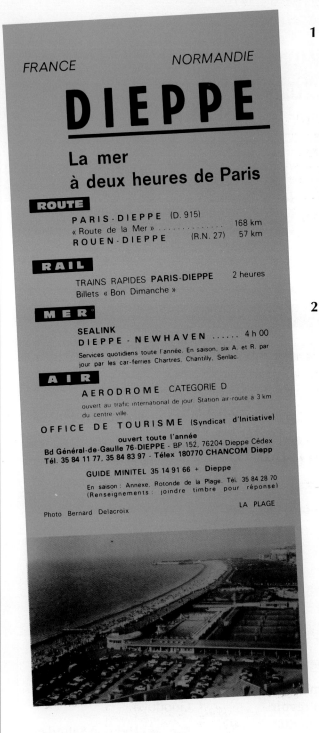

FRANCE   NORMANDIE

DIEPPE

La mer
à deux heures de Paris

ROUTE

PARIS - DIEPPE (D. 915)
« Route de la Mer » .... 168 km
ROUEN - DIEPPE (R.N. 27) 57 km

RAIL

TRAINS RAPIDES PARIS-DIEPPE 2 heures
Billets « Bon Dimanche »

MER

SEALINK
DIEPPE - NEWHAVEN ...... 4 h 00
Services quotidiens toute l'année. En saison, six A. et R. par
jour par les car-ferries Chartres, Chantilly, Senlac.

AIR

AERODROME CATEGORIE D
ouvert au trafic international de jour. Station air-route à 3 km
du centre-ville.

OFFICE DE TOURISME (Syndicat d'Initiative)
ouvert toute l'année
Bd Général-de-Gaulle 76-DIEPPE - BP 152, 76204 Dieppe Cédex
Tél. 35 84 11 77, 35 84 83 97 - Télex 180770 CHANCOM Diepp

GUIDE MINITEL 35 14 91 66 + Dieppe
En saison : Annexe, Rotonde de la Plage. Tél. 35 84 28 70
(Renseignements : joindre timbre pour réponse)

LA PLAGE

Photo Bernard Delacroix

1 Lisez et complétez

a La route Paris–Dieppe s'appelle 'La route _____
_____ _____'.

b Dieppe est à 57 km de _____ .

c Paris est à _____ heures de Dieppe par le
train.

d Newhaven est _____ _____ heures de
Dieppe.

e La station air-route est _____ _____ _____
du centre-ville.

f L'adresse de l'Office de Tourisme est

_____
_____
_____

2 On arrive à Dieppe

Réponds aux questions:

a Stephanie Durel habite Rouen.
Elle va à Dieppe en voiture.
Elle prend quelle Route Nationale?

b Jean-Marc Estivant habite Paris.
Il va passer son dimanche à Dieppe.
Il préfère voyager par le train.
Le voyage Paris–Dieppe dure combien de temps?

c Susan Phillips habite Newhaven.
Elle arrive à Dieppe en bateau.
Elle quitte Newhaven à 16h 00.
Elle arrive à Dieppe à quelle heure?

d Franz et Martine Laroche habitent Genève, en
Suisse.
Est-ce qu'ils peuvent aller à Dieppe en avion?

Mots-clés 4

en voiture	by car
par le train	by train
en bateau	by boat
en avion	by air

3 Distances

Exemple:

'Dieppe est à quelle distance de Paris?'
'Dieppe est à cent soixante-huit kilomètres de Paris.'

CAEN

170	DIEPPE			
767	723	GENEVE		
1005	952	434	MARSEILLE	
240	168	537	776	PARIS
124	57	666	904	111	ROUEN

Mots-clés 5

100	**cent**	1000	**mille**
101	**cent un**	1035	**mille trente-cinq**
200	**deux cents**	7000	**sept mille**
350	**trois cent cinquante**		
999	**neuf cent quatre-vingt-dix-neuf**		

Pour rire: Un remède contre l'insomnie?

85

Oui, tu peux!

Pouvoir

You've seen that in France you can buy stamps at a tobacconist's:

> **En France, on peut acheter des timbres dans un bureau de tabac.**

In Dieppe, you can visit the castle …

> **A Dieppe, on peut visiter le château...**

… or bathe in the sea.

> **...ou se baigner dans la mer.**

To say you can do things, use the verb **pouvoir**:

je peux	I can	**nous pouvons**	we can
tu peux	you can	**vous pouvez**	you can
il/elle peut	he/she can	**ils/elles peuvent**	they can

1 Les panneaux

You can sometimes spot bits of **pouvoir** on notices:

a This warning is often seen near railway level crossings. **Cacher** is 'to hide', so what do you think the message is?

b This anti-vandal notice is on the door of a telephone box. **Un coup de fil** is a phone call; **une vie** is a life. Can you work out what the message means?

c This sign in Caen tells motorists about a new way of paying at parking meters. **Stationnement** is 'parking'. What do you think the message is?

2 Je peux...?

Imagine you're staying at a French friend's house.
Using **Je peux** and the words in the question mark, ask if you can

a watch television
b go to the cinema
c listen to the radio
d buy a postcard
e visit the castle
f play tennis.

Now ask if you can

g visit the port
h buy an ice cream
i play football
j help
k go to the market
l choose a tee-shirt.

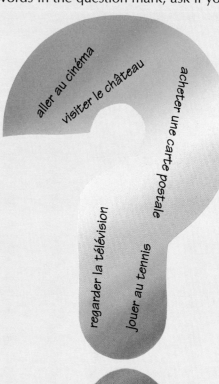

Non, tu ne peux pas!

As elsewhere, you'll find signs and notices in France telling you that certain things are forbidden.

You'll often see the words

INTERDIT (DE) and **DEFENSE (DE)**

Sometimes they come in a slightly longer form:

IL EST (FORMELLEMENT) INTERDIT DE...
It is (strictly) forbidden to …

The top part of this notice is telling you not to dump rubbish.

1 **Lisez**

Who or what is 'forbidden' in each of the following?

a
IL EST INTERDIT
de laisser les chiens
en liberté dans
LE PARC

b
INTERDIT
aux enfants
non accompagnés

d
Danger
Il est interdit au public
de traverser les voies.

Empruntez
le passage souterrain.

c
Défense Absolue
de STATIONNER
Sortie
de MOTO

f
INTERDIT AUX
CYCLES-MOTOS,
et VOITURES

e
Il est interdit de
monter sur les remparts
sous peine de
procès verbal

g
PLAGE
INTERDITE
A TOUS LES
ANIMAUX

2 Complétez

Utilise le verbe **pouvoir** et **ne...pas** pour compléter les phrases.

Exemple: *On ne peut pas laisser les chiens*
en liberté dans le parc.

a On _____ laisser les chiens en liberté dans le parc.
b Les enfants non accompagnés _____ entrer.
c Vous _____ stationner.
d Le public _____ traverser les voies.
e On _____ monter sur les remparts.
f Vous _____ circuler en voiture sur la plage.
g Les animaux _____ aller sur la plage.

★ 3 **Lisez**

Here are three longer notices. How much of each can you work out?

a

ALLÉE RÉSERVÉE
AUX PIÉTONS

SUR L'ENSEMBLE DU BOULEVARD
LE STATIONNEMENT N'EST TOLÉRÉ QUE
POUR LES VOITURES DE TOURISME, IL EST
INTERDIT POUR LES AUTRES VÉHICULES
ARRÊTÉ MUNICIPAL DU 23·00·1974

b

JARDIN PUBLIC

- La circulation en vélo doit se
faire avec la plus grande prudence.
- Les chiens doivent obligatoirement
être tenus en laisse.
- La circulation des engins à
moteurs est formellement interdite.

c

ZONE PIÉTONNE
LIVRAISONS AUTORISÉES
DU LUNDI AU VENDREDI
DE 0h À 10h
DE 20h À 24h
LE SAMEDI DE 0h À 7h

Interdit aux voitures
et aux motos
Les vélomoteurs et les vélos
doivent être tenus à la main
Les chiens doivent être
tenus en laisse

Renseignements

Photo Bernard Delacroix

LE GOLF MINIATURE
ET LE VIEUX CHATEAU

Au creux de la vallée de l'Arques

DIEPPE

ouvert largement sur la mer

VILLE (40.000 habitants) animée en toutes saisons et riche d'un passé que le touriste retrouve sur la belle façade de Saint-Jacques, sur la robuste silhouette de son Vieux Château, ou dans la riche collection de ses ivoires présentés au Musée. Grande-Rue piétonne, marché pittoresque le samedi. Importante Bibliothèque. Animations culturelles. Six salles de cinéma. Centre d'Actions Culturelles Jean Renoir.

PORT Très actif : Pêche fraîche de poisson de qualité ; ligne de car-ferries Dieppe-Newhaven pour voyageurs et marchandises ; navires porte-conteneurs Dieppe-Shoreham ; cargos d'agrumes du Maroc ; bananes des Antilles et d'Afrique ; espace pour plaisanciers ; promenade en mer et pêche au lancer.

PLAGE doyenne de France, c'est une station climatique réputée pour son atmosphère iodée si salubre (thalassothérapie toute l'année). Pour les touristes, Dieppe a tous les attraits d'une grande station moderne :
Casino (ouvert toute l'année : boule roulette, baccara, jeux américains, théâtre, cinéma), piscine olympique d'eau de mer chauffée (24°), tennis (10 courts), golf (18 trous), golf miniature, parc Jehan-Ango et vastes jardins d'enfants gratuits, voile, planche à voile, hippodrome (10 réunions), équitation, pétanque, tir au pigeon, tir à l'arc, plan pour mise à l'eau des dériveurs.
VASTE PARKING EN BORDURE DE MER

DIEPPE

à mi-chemin entre Londres et Paris

1 Help!

Look through the **VILLE** and **PLAGE** sections of the brochure and try to answer this visitor's enquiries about Dieppe ...

a What can you see at the museum?
b What day is the market held on?
c If the weather's bad, will I have a good choice of films to see?
d Could you give me some information about the swimming pool?

e I love tennis and golf. Is there anything here for me?

2 Dieppe: an introduction

Using the information you gathered from **Bienvenue à Dieppe** (page 84) and from this page of the tourist brochure, write an information sheet about Dieppe that you think would be helpful to a first-time visitor to the town who doesn't know any French.

Au château

1 Lisez

Tu décides de monter au Vieux Château. Mais...il y a un problème?
Non! Regarde bien...

- Si tu montes à pied, qu'est-ce que tu fais?

- ...et si tu montes en voiture?

2 Ecoutez: Vrai ou faux?

Au château, il y a un musée. Est-ce que tu peux entrer?

- Regarde les renseignements.

- Ecoute bien les neuf phrases.

- Ecris V (vrai) ou F (faux) pour chacune.

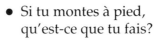

Au château, on a une vue
panoramique de la mer,
de la plage, des pelouses, de la
piscine, des courts de
tennis...(à suivre)

Loterie

Ecoutez

Voici une liste des prix...

a un vélo
b 10 bouteilles de vin
c une calculatrice
d un radio-cassette
e une bouteille de champagne

f une boîte de chocolats
g un tee-shirt
h deux places de cinéma
i un stylo
j deux poissons rouges.

Maintenant, regarde la liste, écoute bien et écris le numéro du ticket gagnant.

★ **Mots croisés**

Cette fois, c'est à toi de trouver les définitions!

Exemple:

Verticalement, 2: On va à l' _____ le dimanche.

Horizontalement:
1
4
5
7
10
11

Verticalement:
2
3
5
6
8
9

	¹M	I	L	L	²E			³M
					⁴G	A	R	E	R
	⁵T	A	⁶B	A	C	L		R
	R		A			I		
⁷C	A	R	T	E	⁸P	O	S	T	A	⁹L	E
	I		E		L	E		O
	N		A		A		¹⁰H	U	I	T
	U		G				N
	⁹¹C...						

Le jeu des dix erreurs

En recopiant son dessin original, l'artiste a fait dix erreurs. Peux-tu trouver ces dix erreurs dans le dessin modifié?

Exemple: Sur le dessin original, il y a une moto.

Sur le dessin modifié, il y a deux motos.

DESSIN ORIGINAL

DESSIN MODIFIE

FRANCE INFO: La Poste

1 Les adresses

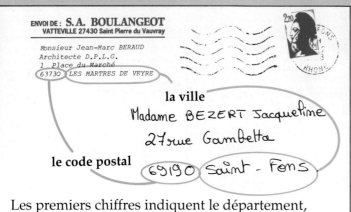

Les premiers chiffres indiquent le département,
par exemple: 63 = Puy-de-Dôme   69 = Rhône

5

Many French people, especially those who live in flats, have a mail box to receive their post (**le courrier**).

What is this PTT advert about?

LA POSTE

La nouvelle boîte aux lettres.
Adoptez la nouvelle boîte aux lettres pour recevoir tout votre courrier en bon état.

26 cm
34 cm
26 cm

2 Les boîtes aux lettres

RF = République Française

POSTES
heures des levées
NE PAS JETER DE JOURNAUX DANS CETTE BOÎTE

On peut poster des lettres dans la boîte. On peut poster des cartes postales dans la boîte. Mais IL EST INTERDIT de poster _____ dans la boîte.

L'oiseau bleu, emblème de la Poste. Si tu cherches un bureau de poste, cherche les lettres **PTT**...et l'oiseau bleu, bien sûr!

LA POSTE
PTT

La Poste
(Postes, Télégraphes, Téléphones)

4 Le facteur

3

En France, les boîtes aux lettres sont jaunes. Et les camionnettes?

Es-tu bon détective?

You can learn a lot from envelopes … if you know where to look!

Unité 7

On s'amuse à Dieppe!

When you've finished unit 7 you'll be able to

- talk about sports and entertainments
- discuss what you want and don't want to do
- make a journey by train
- say what you have done or have been doing.

Les sports

1 Regardez et écoutez

A Dieppe, il y a beaucoup d'activités sportives. Qu'est-ce qu'on peut faire?

On peut nager dans la mer, faire de la voile ou de la planche à voile.

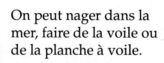

Sur les pelouses, on peut jouer au football et faire de l'équitation.

On peut se baigner dans la piscine,

...on peut jouer au tennis,

...on peut jouer au mini-golf.

Mots-clés 1

nager	to swim
se baigner	to bathe
la voile	sailing
la planche à voile	windsurfing
l'équitation (f)	horse-riding
une piscine	swimming pool
une pelouse	lawn, grassy area
jouer (au football)	to play (football)
faire (de la	to go (windsurfing)
planche à voile)	

Tu te rappelles?

jouer to play

je joue
tu joues
il/elle joue
nous jouons
vous jouez
ils/elles jouent

Faire

Faire is used with lots of expressions. Usually it means **to make** or **to do**.
But you've also met **il fait beau** – what does it mean?

Here are all the parts of **faire**:

je fais	**nous faisons**
tu fais	**vous faites**
il/elle fait	**ils/elles font**

2 On s'amuse...en classe!

Ces élèves de 5ᵉ travaillent en classe. Mais dans leur imagination ils sont en vacances à Dieppe. Qu'est-ce qu'ils font?

Exemple:

a Muriel joue au tennis.

a Muriel **b David** **c Renaud** **d Yamina**

e Carole **f Amadou** **g Myriam** **h Félix**

3 Répondez: Sports divers à Dieppe

1

> Quand il fait du soleil, j'aime faire de la planche à voile.

> C'est sensationnel!

a Quel temps fait-il?
b Que fait le garçon?
c Est-ce qu'il aime ce sport?

2

> Quand nous sommes en vacances, nous préférons jouer au football. C'est notre sport favori.

a Que font les garçons?
b Où sont-ils?
c Combien de joueurs y a-t-il?

3

> Il fait chaud aujourd'hui. On se baigne dans la mer?

> Tu es complètement fou! L'eau est trop froide. On va à la piscine. Elle est chauffée.

a Quel temps fait-il?
b La mer, elle est chaude?
c Où vont-ils se baigner?

4

> Ah non, monsieur-dame. Cette jeune fille n'est pas Blanche-Neige! C'est aujourd'hui mardi, alors Blanche-Neige joue au rugby avec mes six camarades!

a Que fait la jeune fille sur la photo?
b Quel jour sommes-nous?
c Que fait Blanche-Neige en ce moment?

Et toi!

a Quand il fait beau, quel sport aimes-tu faire?
b Quel est ton sport favori?
c Préfères-tu nager dans la mer ou dans une piscine?
d Aimes-tu le mini-golf?

Qu'est-ce qu'on va faire?

1 Ecoutez

Voici un groupe de jeunes sur la promenade à Dieppe.
Ils décident comment passer l'après-midi.
Ecoute la conversation. C'est Martine qui parle la première...

Michel

Martine

Joëlle

Sophie

LE GLOOPi
PARC DE LOISIRS
AUZOUVILLE SUR SAANE
tél. 35 83 23 47

RESTAURANT
BANQUETS -
CEREMONIES

Ouvert du 2 Avril au 15 Octobre, de 10 h à 20 h
Vous trouverez à votre service :

Cette carte vaut
5F00
DE REDUCTION
valable sur une
entrée au parc
SAISON
1988
GAGNEZ DES VOYAGES !

ROUEN
normandie
france

REX — 35 84 22 74

Mar., 20 h 45 « Dernière soirée »
CORENTIN

Mar., 15 h, 20 h 45 - Mer., Jeu., 15 h, 20 h 45
KARATE TIGER

Mar., 15 h, 20 h 45 - Mer., 15 h - Jeu., 15 h
**LE RETOUR DES
MORTS VIVANTS - 2**
Film de Ken Wiederhorm

Mer., 20 h 45 - Jeu., 20 h 45
L'EMPRISE DES TÉNÈBRES
Film de Wes Craven

Connaissez-vous... **CLUB 5**

ce qu'il vous offre...
Jouez au
TENNIS et au SQUASH
du 1er Janvier au 31 Décembre

• **Faire de la**
GYM et du YOGA
avec des professeurs diplômés

• **Garder sa**
FORME et son BRONZAGE
grâce aux bancs et U.V.A

Tout cela c'est maintenant possible...
à DIEPPE chemin des Vertus
(Près du Château d'Eau)

35 84 00 04

Vouloir

To say you'd like to (go to the cinema), use
je voudrais (aller au cinéma)
To say you want to (play squash), use
je voudrais (jouer au squash)
To say something's all right by you, use
je veux bien

Je veux comes from **vouloir**:

je veux	nous voulons
tu veux	vous voulez
il/elle veut	ils/elles veulent

Mots-clés 2

trop chaud	too hot	**être d'accord**	to agree
trop de monde	too many people	**d'accord!**	OK!
quelle horreur!	how horrible!	**passer (un film)**	to show (a film)
bon alors	right then		
on pourrait...	we could …		
moi aussi	me too	**passer (l'après-midi)**	to spend (the afternoon)

2 Ecoutez

Ecoute encore une fois la conversation et réponds à la question **Qui...?**

a Qui voudrait jouer au squash?
b Qui veut visiter 'le Gloopi'?
c Qui veut aller au cinéma?
d Qui préfère passer l'après-midi à Rouen?

3 Pourquoi?

a Why are these suggestions turned down?

- playing squash
- going to the fun park
- going to see a film

b Why do all the friends agree to go to Rouen?

c Explique **a** et **b** en français, en employant **parce que** (because).

4 A deux: Parce que...

Toi et ton/ta partenaire, vous êtes en vacances à Dieppe...

- Regardez les distractions (page 99, Le Club 5, etc.).
- Décidez comment vous allez passer l'après-midi.
- Expliquez votre décision à la classe.

Exemple:

'Nous allons passer l'après-midi au Gloopi, parce que nous aimons les jeux.'

5 Puzzle: Le sport caché

- Trouve les noms de six sports ou distractions (colonnes verticales).
- Tu vas trouver le nom d'un sport caché dans une des rangées horizontales.
- C'est quel sport?

ISSN 0751-6002

Je cherche un(e) correspondant(e)

Voici quatre petites annonces parues dans un magazine de jeunes: les filles/garçons cherchent des correspondant(e)s...

ANNE MICHAUD, 85 rue de l'Hôpital, 9244, Diekirch, Luxembourg. Je cherche un(e) correspondant(e) entre 12–14 ans qui aime les chevaux et qui fait de l'équitation.

MARIE FATET, 21 quai des Bergues, Genève, Suisse. Je voudrais correspondre avec filles ou garçons qui aiment la voile.

JEAN-MARC POCHAT, 32 Dieweg, 1180 Bruxelles, Belgique, cherche correspondant(e) de 12–13 ans, n'habitant pas la Belgique, aimant les sports (football, tennis).

DANIEL ROUGEON, Entrée B, Résidence Place J-Jaurès, 59450 Sin-le-Noble, cherche correspondant(e) en classe de 5e aimant les animaux, la musique, les timbres.

1   Questions

Who (write down the first name) …
a   … likes animals?
b   … lives in Hospital Street?
c   … lives in Switzerland?
d   … is interested in stamps?
e   … wants a correspondent who doesn't live in Belgium?
f   … likes riding?
g   … likes sailing?

2   Ecrivez   ★

Choisis une des annonces. Ecris une réponse.

- J'habite...
- âge/classe
- J'aime...

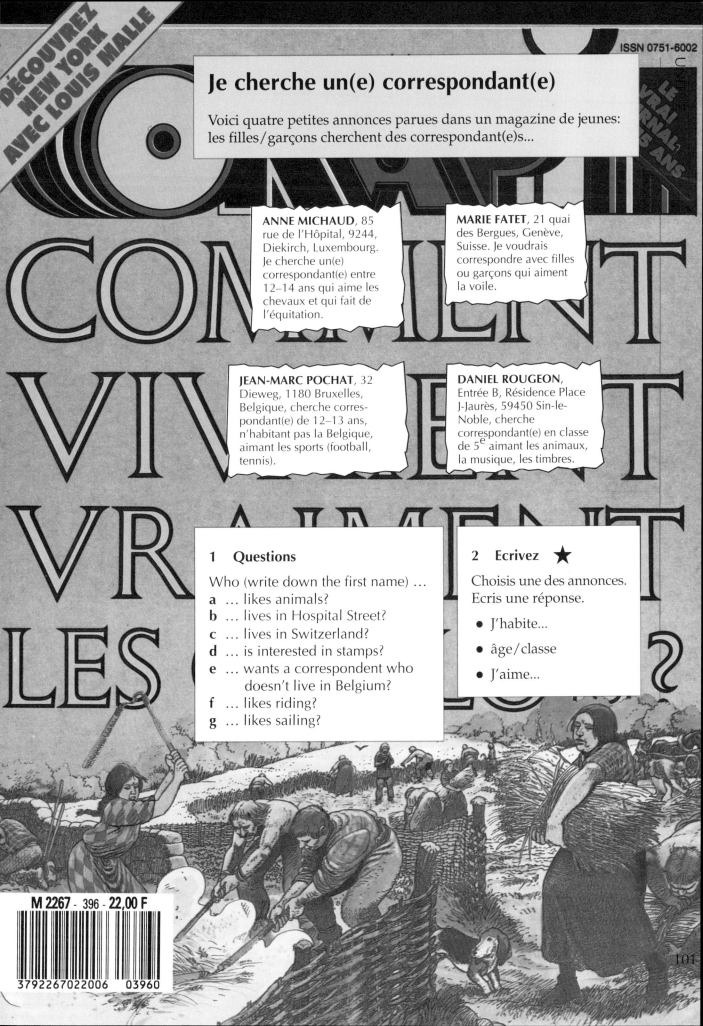

Excursion à Rouen

1 Le départ

Il est une heure: Martine et ses camarades arrivent à la gare de Dieppe. D'abord, ils veulent connaître les horaires des trains pour Rouen...

| 13h 25 | ROUEN | 3 |

Sophie va consulter les horaires:
'Le prochain train pour Rouen part à treize heures vingt-cinq. Bon, on a vingt-cinq minutes à attendre. Quel quai?...Euh, le quai numéro trois.'

Michel va au bureau des renseignements:
'Le voyage Dieppe–Rouen dure combien de temps, s'il vous plaît?'
'Cinquante minutes, monsieur. Le prochain train arrive à Rouen à quatorze heures quinze.'

Joëlle va au kiosque à journaux acheter un magazine:
'Vous avez le dernier numéro d'*OK*, s'il vous plaît?'
'Bien sûr, mademoiselle. C'est tout?'
'Non, je voudrais aussi une tablette de chocolat.'

Martine va au guichet prendre les billets:
'Quatre aller-retour pour Rouen, deuxième classe, s'il vous plaît.'
'Voilà, mademoiselle. 180 francs.'

Mots-clés 3

la gare	station	**le train pour (Rouen) part/arrive à**	
un horaire	timetable	**quelle heure?**	
le quai	platform	what time does the train to (Rouen)	
le kiosque à	newspaper	leave/arrive?	
journaux	stall	**un aller-retour**	a return ticket
le guichet	ticket office	**un aller (simple)**	a single ticket
le billet	ticket	**deuxième/première**	second/first
le prochain	the next train	**classe**	class
train			

 2 La visite

Rouen, capitale de la Normandie, est une ville très ancienne. Elle est située sur la Seine entre Dieppe (à 57 km) et Paris (à 111 km). C'est une ville historique, avec une cathédrale et de vieilles maisons. C'est aussi un port important.

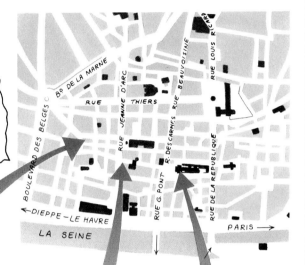

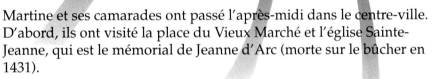

Martine et ses camarades ont passé l'après-midi dans le centre-ville. D'abord, ils ont visité la place du Vieux Marché et l'église Sainte-Jeanne, qui est le mémorial de Jeanne d'Arc (morte sur le bûcher en 1431).

Ils ont fait du shopping dans les rues piétonnes. Ils ont pris des milk-shakes dans un restaurant fast-food.

Ensuite, ils ont acheté des souvenirs et ils ont visité la cathédrale.

A six heures ils ont pris le train pour Dieppe.

Le train pour...

1 Ecoutez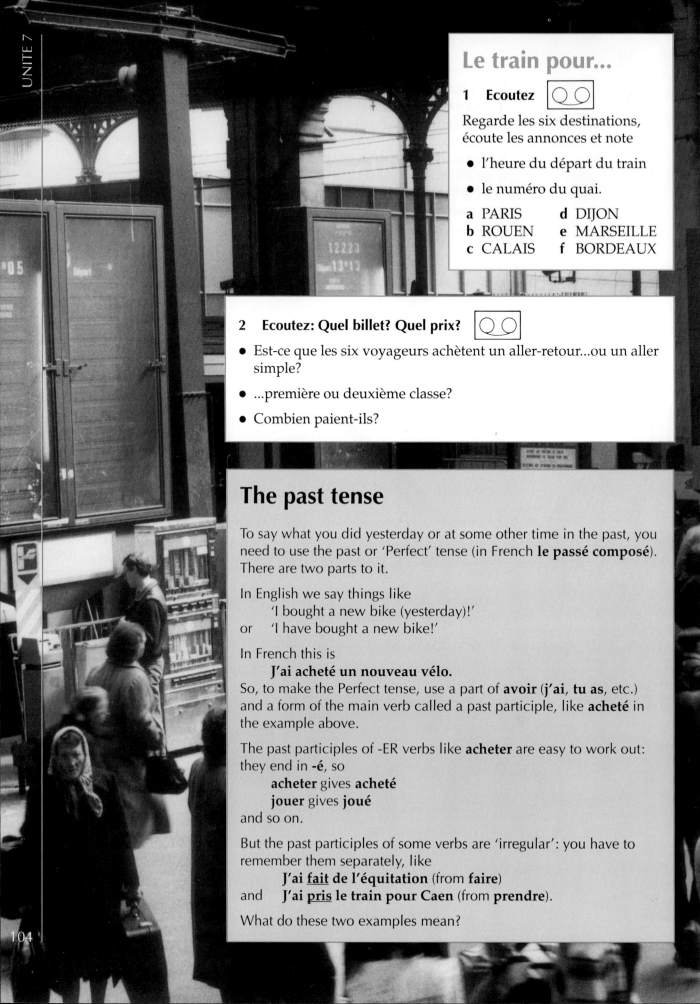

Regarde les six destinations,
écoute les annonces et note

● l'heure du départ du train

● le numéro du quai.

a	PARIS	**d**	DIJON
b	ROUEN	**e**	MARSEILLE
c	CALAIS	**f**	BORDEAUX

2 Ecoutez: Quel billet? Quel prix?

● Est-ce que les six voyageurs achètent un aller-retour...ou un aller
simple?

● ...première ou deuxième classe?

● Combien paient-ils?

The past tense

To say what you did yesterday or at some other time in the past, you
need to use the past or 'Perfect' tense (in French **le passé composé**).
There are two parts to it.

In English we say things like
    'I bought a new bike (yesterday)!'
or   'I have bought a new bike!'

In French this is
    J'ai acheté un nouveau vélo.
So, to make the Perfect tense, use a part of **avoir** (**j'ai**, **tu as**, etc.)
and a form of the main verb called a past participle, like **acheté** in
the example above.

The past participles of -ER verbs like **acheter** are easy to work out:
they end in **-é**, so
    acheter gives **acheté**
    jouer gives **joué**
and so on.

But the past participles of some verbs are 'irregular': you have to
remember them separately, like
    J'ai <u>fait</u> de l'équitation (from **faire**)
and   **J'ai <u>pris</u> le train pour Caen** (from **prendre**).

What do these two examples mean?

Martine

 Sophie

Michel

Joëlle

UNITE 7

3 Lisez et répondez: Qui?

Lis la section *Excursion à Rouen: le départ* et réponds aux questions:

a Qui a consulté les horaires?
b Qui a demandé des renseignements sur le voyage Dieppe–Rouen?
c Qui a acheté un magazine et du chocolat?
d Qui a pris les billets pour Rouen?

4 Lisez et répondez: Qu'est-ce qu'ils ont fait à Rouen?

Lis la section *Excursion à Rouen: la visite* et réponds aux questions:

a Où est-ce que Martine et ses camarades ont passé l'après-midi?
b Qu'est-ce qu'ils ont visité d'abord?
c Où est-ce qu'ils ont fait du shopping?
d Qu'est-ce qu'ils ont pris au restaurant fast-food?
e Qu'est-ce qu'ils ont acheté ensuite?
f A quelle heure ont-ils pris le train pour Dieppe?

★ **5 Ecrivez: Excursion à Rouen: le récit**

● Imagine que tu es Martine ou Michel.

● Ecris une description de ton excursion à Rouen.

● Commence: Hier, nous avons décidé de passer l'après-midi à Rouen...

★ **6 A deux: Bon voyage!**

Rôles:

Partenaire A: touriste
Partenaire B: employé(e) de la SNCF (page 149)

Partenaire A: touriste

● Tu as décidé de faire une excursion en train.

● Choisis ta destination: PARIS   MARSEILLE
                             ROUEN   DIJON
                             CHERBOURG

● Va au guichet et parle à l'employé(e):
  — demande à quelle heure le train pour X part
  — demande à quelle heure il arrive à X
  — achète ton billet (choisis un aller ou un aller-retour)
  — demande le prix du billet et paie
  — demande le numéro du quai.

● Sur un papier note les réponses de l'employé(e).

SNCF
Société Nationale des Chemins de Fer Français

Guide pratique du voyageur

	Période bleue	Période blanche
	en général, du samedi 12 h au dimanche 15 h, du lundi 12 h au vendredi 12 h	en général, du vendredi 12 h au samedi 12 h, du dimanche 15 h au lundi 12 h et quelques jours de fêtes.

1 VOUS AVEZ DÉCIDÉ PRENDRE LE TRAIN. VOUS CHOISISSEZ VOTRE HORAIRE EN PERIODE BLEUE OU BLANCHE.

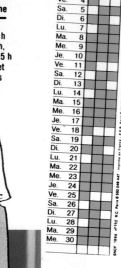

2 VOUS ACHETEZ VOTRE BILLET. N'OU-BLIEZ PAS DE PRENDRE UNE RÉSERVA-TION

Sep. 87		12 h	15 h
Ma.	1		
Me.	2		
Je.	3		
Ve.	4		
Sa.	5		
Di.	6		
Lu.	7		
Ma.	8		
Me.	9		
Je.	10		
Ve.	11		
Sa.	12		
Di.	13		
Lu.	14		
Ma.	15		
Me.	16		
Je.	17		
Ve.	18		
Sa.	19		
Di.	20		
Lu.	21		
Ma.	22		
Me.	23		
Je.	24		
Ve.	25		
Sa.	26		
Di.	27		
Lu.	28		
Ma.	29		
Me.	30		

3 LE JOUR DE VOTRE DÉPART. ARRIVEZ QUELQUES MINUTES EN AVANCE POUR PRENDRE TRANQUILLEMENT VOTRE TRAIN.

ATTENTION : le compostage des billets est obligatoire

- **Introduire chaque billet**
  - face imprimée dessus
  - sous la flèche verte
- **Le glisser vers la gauche jusqu'au déclic**
- **Si la mention "Tournez votre billet" apparaît, présenter l'autre extrémité.**

A la gare...

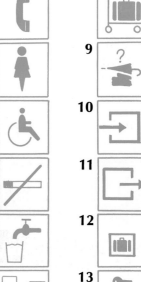

1   8
2   9
3   10
4   11
5   12
6   13
7   14

4 DANS LA GARE, DIRIGEZ-VOUS VERS LE TABLEAU GÉNÉRAL DES TRAINS AU DÉPART POUR REPÉRER LE NUMÉRO DE VOTRE QUAI.

5 N'OUBLIEZ PAS DE COMPOSTER VOTRE BILLET AVANT D'ACCÉDER AU QUAI. C'EST CE QUI REND VOTRE BILLET VALABLE.

Trains au départ

Départ	Destination		Train n°	Voie
14 h 16	BAYEUX - S/LO - COUTANCES FOLLIGNY - PONTORSON - DOL	RENNES	AUTORAIL EXPRESS 1re et 2e CLASSE 3013	8
14 h 32	LISIEUX - BERNAY - EVREUX	PARIS	TURBOTRAIN RAPIDE 1re et 2e classe 3348	1
15 h 01	BAYEUX - LISON CARENTAN - VALOGNES	CHERBOURG	TURBOTRAIN EXPRESS 1re et 2e classe 3309	
15 h 16	SANS-ARRET	PARIS	TURBOTRAIN EXPRESS 1re et 2e classe 3316	
15 h 52	MEZIDON-ARGENTAN-ALENCON LE MANS - CHATEAU DU LOIR	TOURS	EXPRESS 1re et 2e classe 3418	

Départ	De
16 h 12	MEZIDON - LISIEUX - BERN SEROUIGNY-EVREUX-MAN
16 h 25	LISIEUX - EVREUX
16 h 52	BAYEUX
16 h 58	BAYEUX - LISON CARENTAN - VALOGNE
16 h 59	MEZIDON - LISIEUX BERNAY - ELBEUF - S' A
17 h 06	FRENOUVILLE - CAGN MOULT ARGENCES

Accès aux quais ↓   Au-delà de cet votre billet doit compostez-le

Les différents services des grandes gares sont signalés par des dessins.

Ecris le numéro du dessin, puis la lettre correspondant à la bonne définition.

Exemple:

2

Accès aux places

11 à **68**

Non fumeurs

b

Voiture climatisée

c

a **Chariot porte-bagages**

d **Composteurs**

e **Bureau des objets trouvés**

Consigne

j **EAU POTABLE**

Consigne automatique

h **Toilettes pour dames**

i **Sortie**

k **Entrée**

l **Facilités pour handicapés**

m **Bagages**

n **Téléphone public**

Es-tu bon détective?

Daniel, qui habite Paris, a passé quelques jours à Dieppe. Qu'est-ce qu'il a fait? Regarde les images pour le découvrir.

Exemple: Lundi, il a visité le château.

> mardi

> lundi

> mercredi soir

> jeudi matin

> jeudi après-midi

> vendredi matin

> vendredi soi

GOLF de DIEPPE

Route de Pourville
Tél. **35 84 25 05**

créé en 1897

18 trous : 5.716 mètres

Ouvert toute l'année

BAR - RESTAURANT

Fermé le mardi du 1ᵉʳ octobre à Pâques

Demandez le calendrier des compétitions au S.I.

RADIO :

RADIO K 7
STEREO THOMSON MRK 324

FM - PO - GO, témoin lumineux en F.M., auto-stop, piles/secteur.
Garantie : 1 an . . . . **699 F**

LA CABINE

.12 Rue du Mortier d'or.

NOUVEAU choix de

- SALADES COMPOSÉES
- GRATINS
- DESSERTS
- COCKTAILS de JUS de Fruits
- du 15 JUIN au 15 SEPTEMBRE de 12 H à 21H30

DIEPPE - TEL: 35.82.93.93.

EQUITATION SUR LA PLAGE
MICHEL RUBÉ

LEÇONS
VOLTIGE
PROMENADES

PARIS ⇨

Allô météo

Tu es en France...à Dieppe.

Mais...est-ce qu'il va faire beau? Il va faire du soleil, ou est-ce que le ciel va être couvert?

Pour le savoir, appelle le Service d'informations téléphonées de METEO-FRANCE.

36 65 00 00: Cinq jours de prévision du temps sur ta région d'appel.

Pas de problème!

Drôles de situations!

La souris a mangé le chat.

Le poisson a pris le pêcheur.

été 1990 Il a fait beau en Grande-Bretagne.

Unité 8

Au revoir, Dieppe!

When you've finished unit 8 you'll be able to

- find the right shops to buy your presents
- say what's wrong when you're feeling ill
- answer your penfriend's postcard
- unpark a hypermarket shopping trolley!

Alain achète des cadeaux

Alain Moinel habite à Bruxelles, en Belgique. Il passe ses vacances à Dieppe. Mais demain, il va rentrer. Il pense à sa famille...

Grand-père, maman, son ami Vincent, et, bien sûr, son chien, Cactus. Alors...

Il a décidé d'acheter des cadeaux.

D'abord, il a acheté les bonbons...

Merci, madame.

Voilà, monsieur.

Ouf! il fait chaud.

Puis, il a mangé une glace, une glace à la fraise...

Mmm, ça sent bon!

Il a choisi le parfum pour sa mère...

SLOP!
SLIP!

Encore une glace, une glace au citron.

Vous avez choisi, monsieur?

Ensuite, il a cherché un tee-shirt...

SLOP!
SLIP!

Une glace, cette fois une glace à la vanille.

Il a fini par acheter une boîte de Pal. Excellent. Il a juste le temps de...

SLOP!
SLIP!

manger une glace, une glace à la menthe...

Ouuuaaahh! J'ai mal au ventre.

mais, une heure plus tard...

Past tense of -IR verbs

Past participles of -IR verbs end in **-i**, so **finir** gives **fini** and **choisir** gives **choisi**.

As with -ER verbs, you need to put a part of **avoir** in front of the **fini** or the **choisi**, for example:

Tu as fini de manger?
Elle a choisi une glace au chocolat.

Qu'est-ce qu'ils ont choisi?

Exemple: **a** Il a choisi un *stylo*.

Les cadeaux

Delphine passe ses vacances chez son amie Elise. Mais demain, elle va rentrer à la maison. Elle voudrait acheter des cadeaux...

1 Ecoutez et écrivez

a ● Who are the presents for?

● What has she in mind for each person?

b Où peut-elle acheter les cadeaux? Copie le plan. Ecoute ce que dit Elise et dessine les cadeaux à côté des magasins.

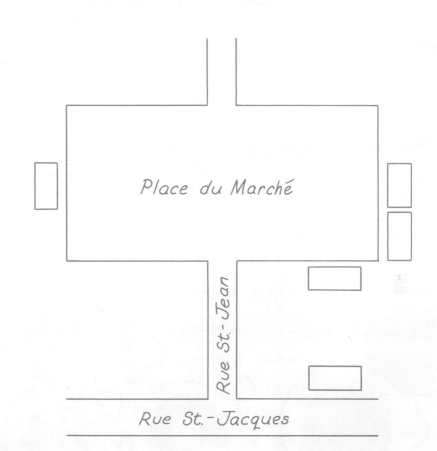

Place du Marché

Rue St.-Jean

Rue St.-Jacques

Mots-clés

en Belgique	in Belgium	**la confiserie**	sweet shop
demain	tomorrow	**la parfumerie**	perfume shop
le cadeau	present(s)	**la pharmacie**	chemist's
(les cadeaux)		**l'épicerie (f)**	grocer's
le bonbon	sweet	**le disque**	record
le parfum	perfume, scent	**la cassette**	cassette

2 Cadeaux de Dieppe

Comme Alain, tu passes tes vacances à Dieppe. Tu veux acheter des cadeaux pour ta famille et pour tes amis. Voici ta liste:

Copy out the list.
Then, against each item on it,
put the letter of the shop or
shops where you might try
to find it.

box of chocolates
tee-shirt
bottle of perfume
pen
jar of jam
tennis balls

a

Spécialités pour lunchs et cocktails

PATISSERIE - CONFISERIE
SALON DE THÉ
SA SUPER GLACERIE

A LA DUCHESSE DE BERRY

Place du Puits-Salé - DIEPPE

Tél. 35 84 21 93

Fabrication exclusivement au beurre

b

MAISON de la PRESSE
JOURNAUX ET PUBLICATIONS
LIBRAIRIE - PAPETERIE
102, Grande-Rue - DIEPPE
TEL. 35 84 33 93
LIBRAIRIE DE LUXE
Stylos Parker, Waterman, etc...

c

INTERSPORT **LaHutte**

VÊTEMENTS - SPORT - CAMPING
ÉQUIPEMENTS COLLECTIVITÉS
168, Grande-Rue - 76200 DIEPPE - Tél. 35 84 80 27

d

H. RATEL

l'artisan chocolatier

115, Grande-Rue, DIEPPE - Tél. 35 84 27 75

Ses spécialités : LE BOUCHON NORMAND
LE PECHE
LE GALET

e

l'épicier
Olivier

16, rue St-Jacques
76200 DIEPPE
Tél. 35 84 22 55

f

VOTRE « PARFUMERIE »

GUERLAIN
HERMES
CHANEL
SAINT-LAURENT
E. LAUDER
etc...

WINDSOR
1-bis, Grande-Rue. 76200 DIEPPE
(près des Arcades)

g

Bouillon CONFISERIE du CASINO
46, rue de la Barre
76200 DIEPPE - Tél. 35 82 14 88

Spécialiste de Chocolats et Dragées

ENGLISH SPOKEN

h

PALAIS DU VÊTEMENT

90, GRANDE-RUE
DIEPPE

Prêt-à-Porter Hommes - Dames
UN ATOUT GAGNANT
La Carte Palais du Vêtement

| PAIEMENT | REMISE 7 % | CREDIT | SERVICE CLIENT |

… and if on your shopping trip you felt like an ice cream, which one of the shops would you go to?

113

Au secours!

Alain, qui a mangé trop de glaces, a mal au ventre. Il va à la pharmacie.

Lisez et écoutez

Alain	Ouahh, j'ai mal au ventre. Je vais consulter le pharmacien.
Pharmacien	Bonjour, jeune homme. Je peux vous aider?
Alain	Ah, oui.
Pharmacien	Qu'est-ce qui ne va pas?
Alain	J'ai mal au ventre...très mal.
Pharmacien	Tenez, voici un médicament spécial. Prenez deux cuillerées avant de manger. Dans deux jours, ça va aller mieux.
Alain	Ah merci, monsieur. Au revoir.
Pharmacien	Au revoir, et attention aux glaces!

Ouahh, je suis malade!

To say you have something the matter with you, use **j'ai mal...**

To say where the problem is, add the part of your body, as in the examples below. Some possible remedies are also given:

Les problèmes

j'ai mal
- au bras — arm
- au pied — foot
- au genou — knee
- au ventre — stomach
- au doigt — finger
- au cou — neck
- au coeur — I feel sick
- à l'oreille — ear
- à la jambe — leg
- à la tête — head
- à la cheville — ankle
- aux yeux — eyes
- aux dents — I've got toothache

Les remèdes

- **de l'aspirine/ un cachet d'aspirine** — aspirin
- **un médicament** — medicine
- **du sparadrap** — sticking plaster
- **un pansement** — bandage, dressing
- **une pommade** — cream, ointment
- **une cuillerée de** — a spoonful of
- **un tube de** — a tube of
- **je vais vous donner...** — I'll give you …
- **je vais vous mettre (un pansement)** — I'll put (a bandage) on it for you

A la pharmacie

Ecoutez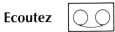

A la Pharmacie Villeneuve à Dieppe, cinq personnes viennent consulter le pharmacien:

a Madame Astruc
b Monsieur Bonnard
c Christophe
d Dorine
e Monsieur François.

- Où ont-elles mal?

- Qu'est-ce que le pharmacien leur donne?

Les pharmacies

Chemists' shops in France (**les pharmacies**) often have a sign in the form of a green cross. Inside the cross are the serpent and staff, which have been symbols of healing since the days of ancient Greece. The same symbols, but in blue, can be seen outside vets' surgeries.

Qu'est-ce qui ne va pas?

Pour Madame Cassetout, ça ne va pas très bien. Pour son chien
Casimir non plus!

1 Ecrivez

Où a-t-elle mal?

a Fais la liste de ses problèmes.
b Puis fais la liste pour Casimir.

Exemple: Elle a mal au genou.

  2 A deux: J'ai mal!

> **Partenaire A:** Tu es en vacances à Dieppe, mais aujourd'hui ça ne
> va pas.
>
> - Décide où tu as mal (au genou, à l'oreille, etc.)
>
> - Va consulter le pharmacien/la pharmacienne de
>   la Pharmacie Villeneuve.

> **Partenaire B:** Tu es le pharmacien/la pharmacienne.
>
> - Un(e) touriste vient te consulter.
>
> - Décide quel remède tu vas donner au/à la
>   touriste.

★ 3 **Chez le vétérinaire**

Imagine que tu es Madame Cassetout.
Ton chien Casimir est malade.
Tu vas consulter M. Corneille, le vétérinaire.
Imagine la conversation.

-X words

In *Alain achète des cadeaux* you saw that 'presents' is **cadeaux**.
Words that end in **-al**, **-eau**, **-eu** and **-ou** usually have **-x** in the plural.

Here are some common ones on signs:

a What do the signs mean?
b What is the singular form of each **-x** word (e.g. **châteaux → un château**)?

A l'hypermarché

Avant de rentrer en Angleterre, tu veux acheter quelques provisions?
Un camembert, par exemple, une boîte de chocolats ou un pot de
confiture?
Alors, tout près de Dieppe, il y a un grand hypermarché Mammouth.

Tu arrives...

Avant d'entrer, tu cherches un chariot.
Où sont-ils? Ah, oui...voilà une dame qui prend
un chariot.

Mais...qu'est-ce qu'on fait?
Regarde bien...

Une pièce de 10F

Alors, tu entres dans l'hypermarché, tu achètes tes provisions et, 'après ton marché', tu quittes le parking...

...en route!

mammouth vous remercie de votre visite

Questions

1 **a** What do you think **Mammouth vous souhaite la bienvenue** means? (Before looking in the vocabulary, think what you might see at the car park entrance to a British hypermarket.)

b To get a shopping trolley, what's the first thing you must do?

c What do you do next?

d Once you have returned the trolley, what's the last thing you are told to do?

e What do you think the sign at the car park exit means?

f What does **RF** on the coin stand for?

PLACE DE LA LIBERTÉ

'Your', 'our' and 'their'

On the signs you saw <u>votre</u> marché, <u>votre</u> visite and <u>vos</u> 10F.
When you speak to someone as **vous** (not **tu**), 'your' will be **votre**
or **vos**.

For example, you might say to your teacher:
> **'J'aime votre pull, mademoiselle!'**
> **'Vos chaussures sont formidables, monsieur!'**

So, when do you use **votre** and when **vos**?

Notre/nos ('our') and **leur/leurs** ('their') work in the same way.

---

2 Les phrases mélangées

Regarde les premières parties des phrases (colonne A), puis choisis la
deuxième partie de chaque phrase (colonne B) pour faire une phrase
complète.

Exemple: 1 *c*

A	B
1 Vous allez récupérer	**a** notre chien.
2 Elles vont passer	**b** pour acheter leurs provisions.
3 Nous aimons bien	**c** vos 10F.
4 Vous avez mangé	**d** leur chat.
5 Les touristes vont à l'hypermarché	**e** vos cadeaux?
6 Vous avez acheté	**f** votre glace?
7 Ils cherchent	**g** nos cadeaux.
8 Nous avons choisi	**h** leurs vacances à Dieppe.

---

3 Lisez

Find an example of **notre/nos**, **votre/vos** or **leur/leurs** in each of these
six notices. What does each one mean?

a

b

c

d

e

f

4 Ecris-moi, s'il te plaît!

Tu vas quitter Dieppe...mais tu as le temps de répondre à cette carte que tu as reçue de ta correspondante, Julie. Elle passe ses vacances en Angleterre.

Voici une carte postale de Dieppe.
Ecris une réponse à Julie (tes impressions de Dieppe, ce que tu as fait, etc.)

Bonjour!
Je suis en Angleterre, à Bournemouth. C'est fantastique! Nous avons fait beaucoup de choses intéressantes. Il a fait chaud et j'ai nagé... dans la mer! J'ai acheté beaucoup de cadeaux et de souvenirs. Envoie-moi une carte de Dieppe!
Salut, et à bientôt!
Julie

Bonnes vacances!

When you've finished unit 9 you'll
- know the names of lots of countries

and be able to
- talk about your holidays
- book in at a hotel or campsite.

Vive les vacances!

C'est bientôt la fin du trimestre d'été.
Au collège Romain-Rolland à Sartrouville dans la région parisienne, les élèves parlent des vacances.

Où va-t-on d'habitude?
Avec qui?
Qu'est-ce qu'on fait pour s'amuser?

 1   Regardez et écoutez

Coraline

P   **Madrid**

Lisboa ○

E

MA

● **Agadir**

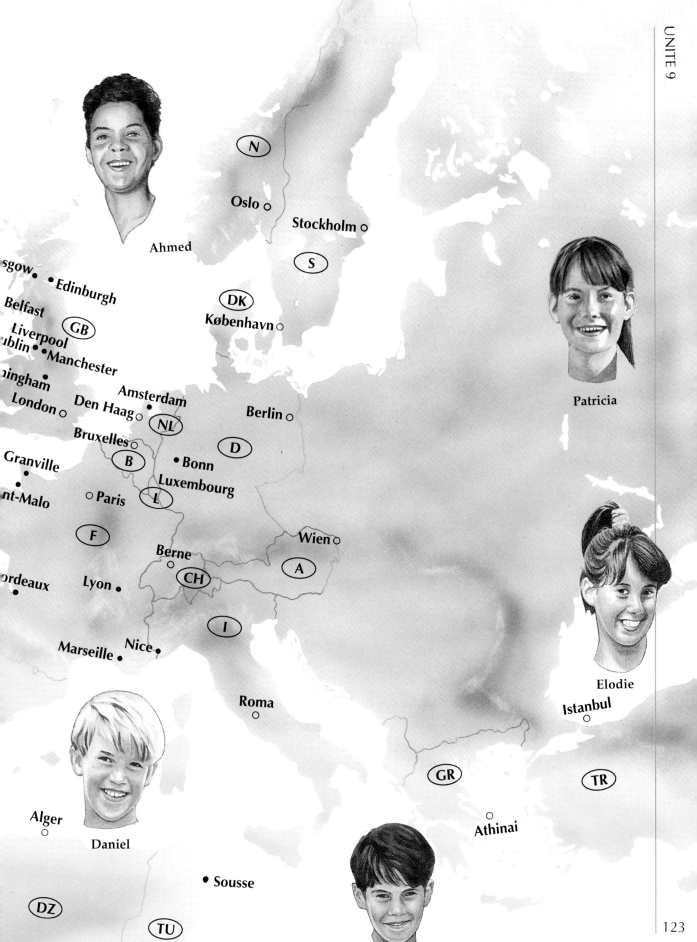

Les pays – countries

- (A) l'Autriche (f)
- (B) la Belgique
- (CH) la Suisse
- (D) l'Allemagne (f)
- (DZ) l'Algérie (f)
- (E) l'Espagne (f)
- (F) la France
- (GB) la Grande-Bretagne
  l'Angleterre (f)
  l'Ecosse (f)
- (GR) la Grèce
- (IRL) l'Irlande (f)
- (I) l'Italie (f)
- (N) la Norvège
- (NL) la Hollande
- (S) la Suède
- (TR) la Turquie
- (TU) la Tunisie

- (DK) le Danemark
- (L) le Luxembourg
- (MA) le Maroc
- (GB) le Pays de Galles
- (P) le Portugal

'To' or 'in' with feminine countries
is **en**:

> 'Où vas-tu?' '<u>En</u> Espagne.'

> Je suis portugais, mais
> j'habite <u>en</u> France.

… but with masculine countries
it's **au**:

> Mohammed envoie une
> carte postale <u>au</u> Maroc.

> Ils habitent à Lisbonne, <u>au</u>
> Portugal.

2 Ecoutez: Où ça?

Dans quel pays est-ce que ces élèves passent leurs vacances?

a Ahmed *passe ses vacances au Maroc.*
b Coraline
c Daniel
d Patricia
e Claude
f Elodie

3 Ecoutez: Où se trouvent les villes?

a Nice *se trouve en France.*
b Lisbonne
c Saint-Malo
d Granville
e Agadir
f Sousse

4 Ecoutez et écrivez: Où vas-tu?

a Where in Morocco does Ahmed say Agadir is situated?
b How does he feel about the town?
c Where does Coraline say Nice is situated?
d How often does she go there?

e Where does Daniel say Portugal is?
f Where does he say Lisbon is situated?
g What else does he say about Lisbon?
h Where does Patricia say Saint-Malo is?
i Does she go there every year?
j Who does she go with?

Mots-clés 1

Où passes-tu tes vacances?	Where do you go for your holidays?
Je passe mes vacances à...	I go to … for my holidays
Je vais/pars en vacances à...	
pendant les/mes vacances	during the/my holidays
les grandes vacances	the summer holidays
les vacances d'été	
au bord de la mer	at/to the seaside
à la campagne	in/to the country
à la montagne	in/to the mountains
Nice se trouve sur la Côte d'Azur	Nice is (situated) on the Côte d'Azur
souvent	often
tous les ans/étés	every year/summer
d'habitude	usually
de temps en temps	from time to time, sometimes
je m'ennuie	I'm bored

5 Ecoutez et écrivez: De temps en temps

Listen again to Claude and Elodie talking about their holidays, and gather as much information as you can about

- where they go
- how often they go there
- what they do
- who they go with or meet
- how they feel about their holiday.

6 A deux: Mes vacances

Voici des questions à poser à ton/ta partenaire au sujet de ses vacances:

Où passes-tu tes vacances?	Qu'est-ce que tu fais pour t'amuser?
C'est où, ça?	Tu vas à...tous les ans?
C'est au bord de la mer?	Quel temps fait-il d'habitude?
Avec qui pars-tu?	Tu aimes bien aller à...?

- D'abord, décidez qui va commencer!
- Choisis cinq questions et pose-les à ton/ta partenaire.
- Note les renseignements qu'il/elle te donne.
- Puis changez de rôle.

D'où viens-tu?

'From' is **de** with feminine countries
and **du** with masculine countries.

So Patricia might say **'Je viens de France'** (I come from France)
Ahmed might say **'Je viens du Maroc'** (I come from Morocco).

'To come' is **venir**:

je viens	nous venons
tu viens	vous venez
il/elle vient	ils/elles viennent

D'où viennent ces touristes?

Exemple:

a 'Il vient d'Italie.'

A l'hôtel

En France, on a un grand choix d'hôtels. Il y a des hôtels de grand luxe, des hôtels à prix modéré (par exemple, les hôtels des chaînes Campanile, Fimotel et Climat de France), et des pensions de famille.

 1 Ecoutez

Quatre touristes arrivent à l'hôtel Les Voyageurs.
Ils parlent à la réceptionniste.

For each tourist, note down

- the kind of room that is booked (e.g. twin-bedded, bath/shower)
- how long it is booked for
- how much it costs
- one other piece of information that is given.

Mots-clés 2

vous avez des chambres libres?	have you any rooms free?
une chambre avec bain/douche/WC	a room with a bath/shower/toilet
pour une nuit/une semaine	for a night/a week
pour deux semaines/quinze jours	for a fortnight
une chambre à un/à deux lits	a single/twin-bedded room
un grand lit	a double bed
c'est combien?	how much is it?
il y a un parking devant/derrière l'hôtel	there's a car park in front of/behind the hotel
l'hôtel ferme à (11h)	the hotel closes at (11 o'clock)
le petit déjeuner est servi à partir de (7h 30)	breakfast is served from (7.30)
le restaurant est ouvert	the restaurant is open

2 À deux: On arrive à l'hôtel

Il y a deux rôles:
Le/La réceptionniste de l'hôtel
Le/La touriste qui cherche une chambre.

réceptionniste	touriste
● Greet the tourist	
	● Ask if there are any rooms free
● Ask how long for	
	● Reply (e.g. a night, two weeks)
● Say what room(s) you have (e.g. with a double bed, twin-bedded)	
	● Ask if they have a bath/shower
● Tell him/her	
	● Ask the price(s)
● Tell him/her	
	● Ask about one other thing (e.g. car park, times of breakfast, restaurant, when hotel closes at night)
● Give the information	

Maintenant, présentez le dialogue à la classe.

3 On quitte l'hôtel

You're coming to the end of your stay in the hotel.

● The food in the restaurant is really good, but it takes a long time to get served and there is quite a wait between courses.

● The self-service breakfast is OK, but if you arrive towards the end, they seem to have run out of some things.

● Your room has a good view and comfortable bed, but the bedside light doesn't work.

● The bathroom is kept very clean.

● Everyone is very friendly and helpful.

● You particularly like the music in the dining room, but you would like some English newspapers.

How will you fill in this form asking for your comments ... and once it's completed, what are you asked to do with it?

Merci de votre passage dans notre hôtel-restaurant 'Climat de France'.

Pour répondre encore mieux à votre attente, nous serions heureux de recueillir vos impressions et suggestions.

● Pouvez-vous noter de 0 à 5:

l'accueil: ☐   les repas: ☐
                le service ☐
la chambre: ☐   la qualité ☐
la salle de bains: ☐   le petit déjeuner ☐
                 buffet

● Appréciations et suggestions:

Si vous le souhaitez, indiquez vos nom et adresse au dos.
Remettre ce questionnaire à la Réception.

4 Bonne nuit!

In your hotel room you found this.
What is it for?

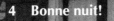

chuttt...

5 Notre hôtel vous offre...

Your neighbours are trying to choose a hotel for a French holiday and
have been sent these details. As they don't speak French, they have
asked you to help them.

Here are their questions. How many answers can you find in the leaflet?

a Is there a phone in the bedroom?
b … and a television?
c Do all the rooms have a bath?
d Is English spoken?
e Are dogs allowed?
f Is there a garden?
g Is there a car park at the hotel?
h Is it a long way from the station?
i Is there a swimming pool?
j Is there a lounge?

Notre Hôtel vous offre

- 2 ★★NN
- 49 Chambres bain ou douche/W.C.
- Centre ville (à 200 m. de la Gare)
- Parking à 50 m.
- Ascenseur
- Pension sur demande
- Veilleur de nuit
- Service en chambre
- Téléphone en chambre
- Salon, télévision et bar
- Nous parlons anglais et allemand
- Chiens admis

Allons faire du camping!

Tu as décidé de faire du camping en France. Tu as choisi la région du sud-ouest, près de Saint-Jean-de-Luz.

Il y a un inconvénient important: c'est loin – loin de Paris, loin de l'Angleterre, alors il y a beaucoup de kilomètres d'autoroute à faire. Tant pis!

Il y a beaucoup d'avantages:

- C'est dans le sud-ouest, alors il fait très chaud, beaucoup plus chaud qu'en Grande-Bretagne.
- C'est près de la frontière espagnole, alors on peut visiter l'Espagne.
- C'est au bord de la mer, alors il y a beaucoup de choses à faire: se baigner, faire du bateau...
- Il y a un grand choix de campings...
- et puis, un camping, c'est moins cher qu'un hôtel!

Maintenant, tu vas choisir un camping!

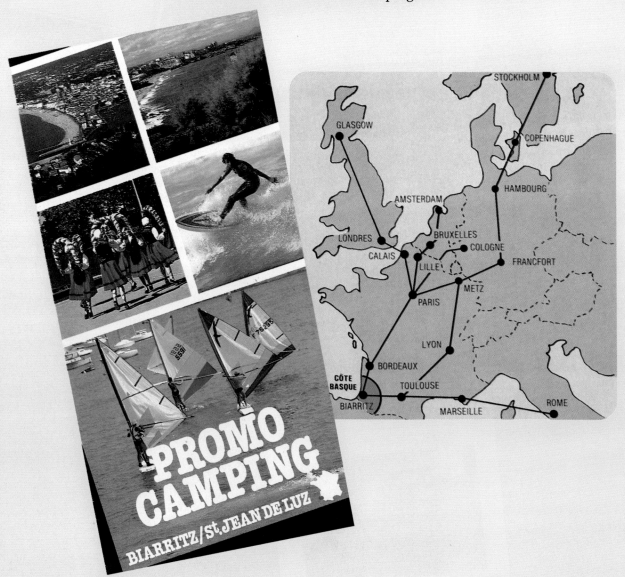

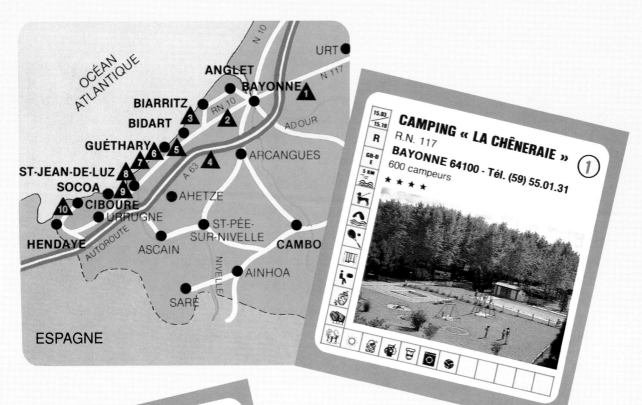

1 Regardez et écrivez

Les trois campings ont chacun un numéro: ① ③ ④
Quel(s) camping(s) choisis-tu...

a si tu aimes les saunas?
b si tu n'aimes pas les chiens?
c si tu veux une piscine?
d si tu veux faire de l'équitation?
e si tu aimes jouer au football?
f s'il y a une personne handicapée dans ta famille?
g si tu veux jouer au golf?
h si tu veux manger au restaurant du camping?

2 Pour réserver un emplacement

Alors, tu as choisi ton camping!
Maintenant, tu vas écrire au directeur du camping pour réserver un emplacement.

D'abord choisis:

- la date de ton arrivée au camping
- la date de ton départ
- le nombre d'adultes dans ton groupe
- le nombre d'enfants (un enfant a moins de 14 ans) et leur âge
- s'il y a une voiture
- si vous avez une tente, une caravane ou une caravane motorisée...
- ...ou si vous voulez louer une tente, etc.

Ecris ta lettre de réservation basée sur la lettre-modèle que voici:

Date

Monsieur le Directeur
Camping ....
at ....

Monsieur le Directeur,
Dear Sir,
Ayant obtenu votre adresse par l'intermédiaire des Services Officiels du Tourisme Français
I have selected your address with the help of the French Government Tourist Office
à Londres, je vous serais obligé de me communiquer rapidement vos conditions et tarifs
in London, and I should be grateful if you would let me know at your earliest convenience
correspondant au séjour suivant:
your conditions for the following stay:

Départ le..
Arrivée le .... Departing on ....
Arriving on ....
Nous sommes..................**adultes et**..................**enfants agés de**..................**ans**
We are ....adults and..................children aged ....years
Nous désirons réserver un emplacement pour une voiture* – tente* – caravane* –
We wish to book a pitch for a car* – tent* – caravan* –

caravane motorisée* **louer une tente* – caravane* – bungalow*** (*delete where not applicable)
motor caravan* hire a tent* – caravan – bungalow*

Veuillez me répondre directement à l'adresse ci-dessous:
Please answer direct to my address below:
Mr/Mrs..
....
....
(block capitals please)

avec mes remerciements,
Yours faithfully,

Au camping: les prix

In France, as in many European countries, campsites are classified according to their facilities. Some are privately owned, but many belong to the town or village and the prices they charge are controlled. The better the site's facilities, the more stars it is awarded and the higher its charges.

CAMPING DE LA PRAIRIE

400 installations   TROIS ÉTOILES   superficie 70 000m2

TARIFS JOURNALIERS
de midi à midi

CAMPEUR (douche chaude comprise)	11^{F}50
ENFANT de moins de 7 ans	5^{F}75
EMPLACEMENT (caravane ou tente + 1 auto)	7^{F}80
VOITURE supplémentaire ou **BATEAU**	4^{F}60
GARAGE MORT du 1er Juin au 15 Septembre	27^{F}10
GARAGE MORT du 16 Septembre au 31 Mai	10^{F}40
ELECTRICITE (9 à 10 ampères maxi) 2000watts	22^{F}15

TAXE DE SÉJOURS: 1F par jour et par personne
0.50F pour les enfants

CAMPEURS AUTORISES 1300

a How many stars does the **Camping de la Prairie** have?

b How many campers is the site allowed to take?

c The charges on the board are for one day. When does the day begin and end?

d What does the daily charge for each camper include?

e For the purposes of campsite charges, when does a person stop being a child?

f How much does it cost per day for one car and a tent?

g What two things cost 4F 60 a day to bring on to the site?

h **Garage mort** is a facility offered to owners of caravans. What do you think it means?

i If there are five people in a group: two adults, two teenagers and a 5-year-old child, how much tax in total will they be charged per day?

2   A deux: L'arrivée

Il y a deux rôles:

　Partenaire A:　Un campeur/Une campeuse qui arrive au Camping
　　　　　　　　　　 La Pinède

　Partenaire B:　Le directeur/La directrice du camping.

D'abord, préparez vos rôles:

Partenaire A: campeur/campeuse Décide ● combien de personnes il y a dans ton groupe (adultes et enfants) ● si vous avez une voiture ● si vous avez une tente ou une caravane ● combien de nuits vous voulez passer au camping.	**Partenaire B:** directeur/directrice ● Regarde la liste des tarifs journaliers du Camping de la Prairie ● Fais une liste similaire pour ton camping (La Pinède), mais change les prix!

Puis jouez vos rôles:

A campeur/campeuse ● Demande s'il y a des emplacements de libre. ● Demande les prix. ● Demande des renseignements supplémentaires, si tu veux (par exemple, s'il y a des douches chaudes, s'il y a une piscine). ● Réponds aux questions du directeur/de la directrice.	**B** directeur/directrice ● Demande combien de campeurs il y a dans le groupe. ● Demande le nombre de nuits qu'ils veulent passer au camping. ● Demande s'ils ont une tente ou une caravane. ● Réponds aux questions du campeur/de la campeuse.

A Chemillé

At the village of Chemillé-sur-Indrois in the Loire Valley, there is a campsite and a man-made lake (**un plan d'eau**) that offers all kinds of facilities for people who like water sports …

1 Lisez

You arrive at the **plan d'eau** and want to know what facilities are on offer:

a In the blue square on the notice, which four activities are mentioned?

b Users of the lake must pay a fee for each of these, even if they have their own equipment. What is the shortest and what is the longest period mentioned?

c What do you think the information in red means?

d **Location** means things can be hired. Apart from a **planche à voile**, what does the notice say you can hire?

e What are the two facilities mentioned at the very bottom of the notice?

Tu aimes faire du pédalo?

2 On fait du pédalo

Voici deux amies qui font du pédalo sur le plan d'eau.
La première amie pose une question. Quelle est la réponse de la deuxième amie?

3 A deux: Décidez!

Tu arrives au plan d'eau avec un(e) ami(e) français(e).
Qu'est-ce que vous allez faire?
Choisissez votre activité préférée…
…puis annoncez-la à la classe.
Donnez aussi les raisons de votre choix.

★ 4 **Ecrivez**

Imagine que tu as passé une journée au plan d'eau de Chemillé.

● Quel temps a-t-il fait?

● Qu'est-ce que tu as fait pour t'amuser?

● As-tu mangé à la buvette, ou as-tu fait un pique-nique?

● A quelle heure as-tu quitté le plan d'eau?

Ecris un petit paragraphe sur ta journée.

Puzzle: Les mots cassés

Mets deux par deux ces groupes de lettres pour trouver des mots relatifs aux vacances:

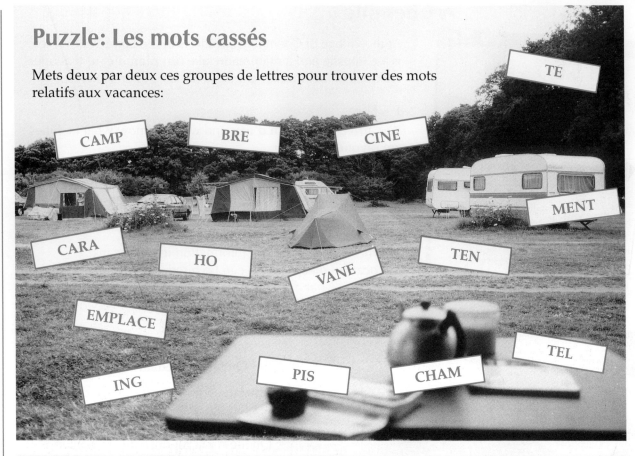

Puzzle: Tu pars avec moi?

NOTRE AMIE VA VISITER CINQ PAYS.
TU PEUX LES TROUVER?
(TOUS DETOURS, RETOURS...
  SONT PERMIS)

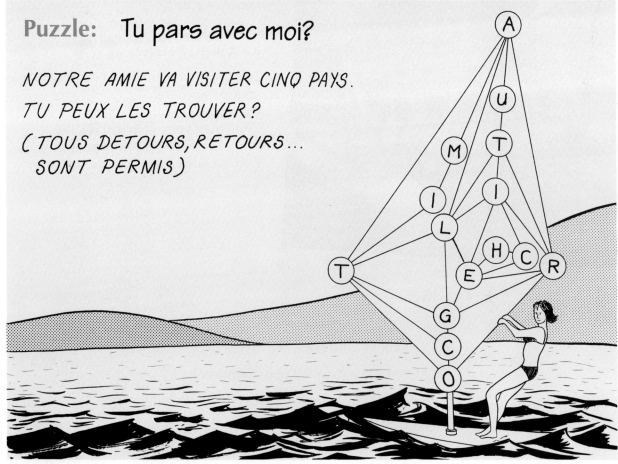

Unité 10

Reprise 2

How much can you remember? In this section you'll have another chance to practise the things you learnt in units 6 to 9 ... and to show how much you know!

Réservation

classe 2

SNCF

| | | Train | 405 | Voiture 07 |
| | 02 | Places | 45, 47 | |

			Prestations	Réduction	Nombre	Prix
Départ	12.30 PARIS NORD					
Arrivée	14.53 BOULOGNE MARITIME					
Date	LE 02.09.86			00	02	
8701600200	Particularités SALLE NON FUMEURS	ASSISE				
203	1FENETRE 1COULOIR					F********* *
000345						
BRITRAILWAYS						
17.07.86 K3						
01408800						
7016 0017 01408800						

Es-tu bon détective?

Using this train reservation as evidence, give as much information as you can about the journey, for example:

● How many people travelled?

● Where did the traveller(s) begin the journey?

● ... and finish it?

● When did the journey take place?

C'est où?

1

Sealink
PASSAGERS · PIETONS
Sealink
↑ 800m

2

Piscine
Eau climatisée
200ᵐ

3

à 800 m ►
chambre
d'hôte

D 197
BERGANTY 1.1 ►

4

HOTEL
RESTAURANT
Terrasse face au lot
Les falaises
☏ 31.26.83.
Traverser le Pont

5

supermarché
champion
les Prix ·
le Choix ·
la Qualité.
à 5 mn
Route de Caen
OUISTREHAM

6

Sentier du Littoral
et Pays de Caux ►
PUYS   :0h45   GR 21
BERNEVAL :3h
(Plage)

7

à 7 mn.
vôtre supermarché
SUPERMARCHE
score
d'accord!

8

HOTEL-RESTAURANT
LE GALESSIE
tél. 65.35.30.27
300 m. à Gauche

9

TERRASSE PANORAMIQUE
HOTEL · RESTAURANT
A 100 METRES DU CASINO   VUE SUR LA MER!
Le Saint-Georges
Tél: 31·97·18·79

1 Quelle photo?

- Ecris les numéros 1–9.
- Ecoute et lis les renseignements, regarde les photos et écris la lettre correspondante.

Exemple: 1 d

a

C'est à gauche, à
trois cents mètres.

b

C'est loin?

Non, c'est tout près...
à sept minutes seulement.

c

Le camping est à gauche,
à deux cents mètres.

d

Pour les voitures, les caravanes
et les camions, c'est à gauche, à
huit cents mètres.

f

C'est loin?

Non, c'est tout près...
à cinq minutes seulement.

e

De la terrasse, vous avez une
vue magnifique sur la mer.

g

C'est à droite, à huit cents
mètres.

h

Berneval, c'est à droite,
à trois heures de marche.

i

Le numéro de téléphone, c'est le trente et un,
vingt-six,
quatre-vingt-trois.

 2 A deux: On se renseigne

Il y a deux rôles:
  Le/La touriste qui cherche son chemin
  Le/La passant(e) qui répond à ses questions et qui donne des renseignements.

- Choisissez vos rôles, choisissez **une** des photos.
- Le/La touriste pose des questions.
  Le/La passant(e) répond.
- Puis...choisissez une autre photo, et changez de rôle.

3 A deux: Dialogue

Cette fois, vous allez travailler ensemble pour préparer un dialogue:

- Choisissez **une** des photos.

Le/La touriste cherche son chemin, mais il/elle pose aussi des questions supplémentaires, par exemple:

- C'est loin?
- C'est à quelle distance?
- C'est un grand hôtel?
- On mange bien dans ce restaurant?
- Quel est le numéro de téléphone?

Le/La passant(e) répond et donne des renseignements supplémentaires, par exemple:

- Il y a une piscine à gauche
- Le casino est à 100m
- Il y a une terrasse
- Puys est à 45 minutes

- Et maintenant...présentez le dialogue à la classe. Bonne chance!

Puzzle: Les deux sacs

Le grand sac contient quatre paires de nombres + un nombre.

Chaque paire, additionnée, = le nombre dans le petit sac...

- Quelles sont les quatre paires?
- Quel est le numéro qui reste?

Puzzle: En vacances!

Passe par certaines lettres pour former les noms de quatre pays.

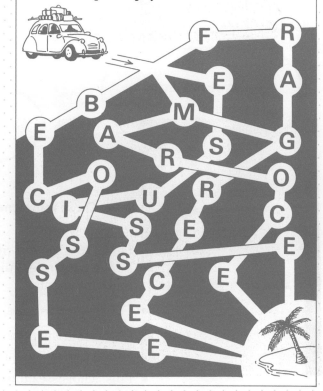

Quatre campings

Lisez

1

2

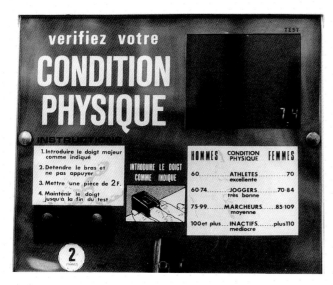

3

4

a In **1**, who are admitted on to the campsite?
b … and who are not admitted?
c In **2**, what are visitors told to do in the left-hand notice?
d … and what does the right-hand notice tell campers?
e In **3**, what does the site have that might attract campers?
f Explain the price list to an English visitor.
g What information is given on sign **4**?

Testez-vous!

a What do you think this machine is for?
b To make it work, you have to do a series of things (1–4 on the left). What are stages 1, 3 and 4?
c In the right-hand section, who should be looking at the numbers on the left … and who at those on the right?
d Who are the four types of people mentioned in the middle of the right-hand section?
e What do you think the numbers on each side indicate?

Comment s'appellent-elles?

Voici dix jeunes filles...elles ont des problèmes, évidemment! Elles s'appellent Anne, Brigitte, Corinne, Diane, Emma, Florence, Gaëlle, Juliette, Madeleine et Nicole.

Regarde les images, puis les phrases en bas.
C'est à toi de trouver l'identité de chacune.

Exemple: Anne = 6

a Anne a mal au ventre et à la tête. Elle n'a pas mal au bras.
b Brigitte n'a pas mal au pied. Elle a mal au genou et elle a aussi mal aux dents.
c Corinne a mal au doigt et elle a mal à l'oreille. Elle n'a pas mal à la cheville.
d Diane n'a pas mal aux yeux, mais elle a mal à la jambe. Au cou, aussi.
e Emma n'a pas mal au ventre, mais elle a mal au bras et à la tête.
f Florence a mal à la tête et à la jambe. Mais elle n'a pas mal aux yeux.
g Gaëlle a mal à l'oreille et au doigt. Elle n'a pas mal à la cheville.
h Juliette a mal au pied et elle a mal aux dents. Elle n'a pas mal au genou.
i Nicole a mal au bras et au ventre. Elle n'a pas mal à la tête.

Mystère: Qui a pris le gâteau?

Ecoutez

Voici un extrait d'un journal...

Un magnifique gâteau a disparu de la Pâtisserie de M. Legros, hier, à 13h 30. On a alerté la police

Il y a quatre suspects:

Félix Fripon

Marie Mensonge

Thomas Trompe

Louise Louche

Le célèbre Inspecteur Indice a posé des questions...

- Ecoute bien.
- Note l'emploi du temps de chaque suspect(e).
- Décide qui n'a pas d'alibi...

143

Un(e) correspondant(e), s'il te plaît!

Voici huit petites annonces parues dans un magazine de jeunes: les filles/garçons cherchent des correspondant(e)s...

SAFIA BENNOUNA, 132 Bd Zertouni, Casablanca, 02 Maroc. Je cherche une correspondante de 12–14 ans aimant la danse, la mode.

JEAN-CLAUDE GUICHARD, chemin du Couchant 17, 1007 Lausanne, Suisse, recherche quelqu'un qui aime la voile et le vélo.

GERARD VACHER, 28 Place de la République, 13013 Marseille, cherche correspondant(e) habitant Angleterre, Ecosse, aimant musique, moto, timbres.

CARINE SOUCHET, 75 rue Casimir Delavigne, 59000 Lille. Je voudrais correspondre avec des jeunes de mon âge (13 ans) qui aiment le cinéma, les voyages.

EMMANUELLE RICHARD, 64 rue du Muguet, 52000 Chaumont, voudrait correspondre avec fille entre 13–15 ans, aimant la nature et adorant les animaux, surtout les chevaux.

FABIENNE RAMIREZ, Santísima Trinidad 62, Barcelona, Espagne, 12 ans ½, cherche correspondant(e) même âge. J'aime la télé, le sport. J'aime aussi les jeux vidéos.

MOHAMMED BOUZID, 9 rue de Batna, Victor-Hugo, 31000 Oran, Algérie, cherche correspondant(e) anglais(e). J'aime nager, jouer au football.

GREGOIRE AUGER, 49 rue Dunois, 75013 Paris. J'ai 13 ans. Je cherche photos et renseignements sur les chats.

e

a

b

c

d

f

g

h

1 Lisez

Which person will each of the following probably choose to write to?

a Martin, who spends hours in front of the TV set

b Emma, who has four cats at home

c Benjamin, who goes sailing every weekend

d Simon, who likes swimming

e Caroline, who wants to be a fashion designer

f Claire, who loves horse-riding

g David, who wants to travel round the world

h Angus, who's mad on motorbikes and collects stamps.

2 Ecrivez

Tu cherches un(e) correspondant(e). Tu mets une annonce dans un magazine français. Qu'est-ce que tu écris?

★ **3 Une réponse**

Which of the eight people would **you** choose to write to? Write a reply, saying how old you are and talking about your house or flat, family and pets. Say what you like doing and ask him or her to write back soon.

La note

On a passé la nuit dans un hôtel. La note arrive...

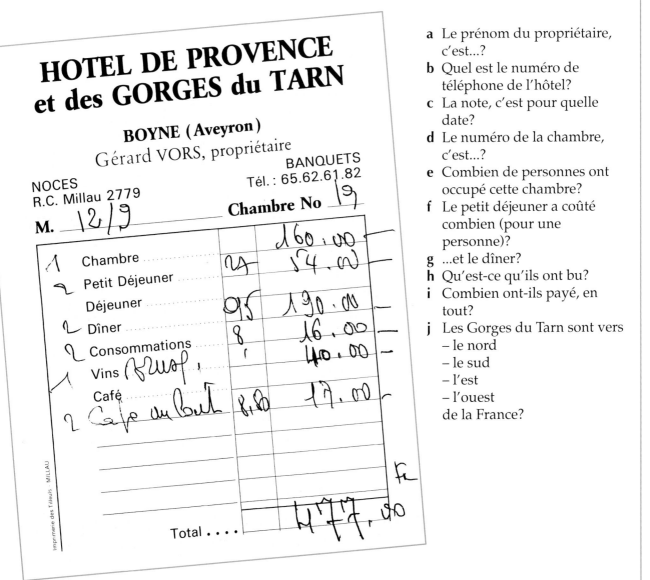

a Le prénom du propriétaire, c'est...?
b Quel est le numéro de téléphone de l'hôtel?
c La note, c'est pour quelle date?
d Le numéro de la chambre, c'est...?
e Combien de personnes ont occupé cette chambre?
f Le petit déjeuner a coûté combien (pour une personne)?
g ...et le dîner?
h Qu'est-ce qu'ils ont bu?
i Combien ont-ils payé, en tout?
j Les Gorges du Tarn sont vers
  – le nord
  – le sud
  – l'est
  – l'ouest
  de la France?

Non!

1 Le code de la route

Ecris le numéro et la lettre du panneau correspondant.

1 Fin de toutes interdictions
2 Interdit aux piétons
3 Défense de faire demi-tour
4 Accès interdit aux cyclistes
5 Stationnement interdit
6 Interdit aux motos
7 Stationnement interdit à gauche les jours impairs, à droite de la route les jours pairs

2 Interdit!

What isn't allowed in each of the following?

3 Complétez

Utilise le verbe **pouvoir** et **ne...pas** pour compléter les phrases.

Exemple: **a** *Le public ne peut pas entrer.*

a Le public _____ entrer.
b Nous _____ stationner.
c Tu _____ circuler à l'intérieur du camp.
d Les chiens _____ aller sur la plage.
e On _____ traverser les voies.
f Les motos _____ circuler dans la zone piétonne.
g Vous _____ faire demi-tour.
h Les caravanes _____ stationner ici.

★ **4 Attention!**

a This notice is on the seashore not far from Dieppe. Can you work out what you musn't do?

b This one is outside a campsite. How much of it can you understand?

Faites des mots

Quelle lettre faut-il mettre, au centre de chaque cercle, pour lire quatre mots dans chacun d'eux?

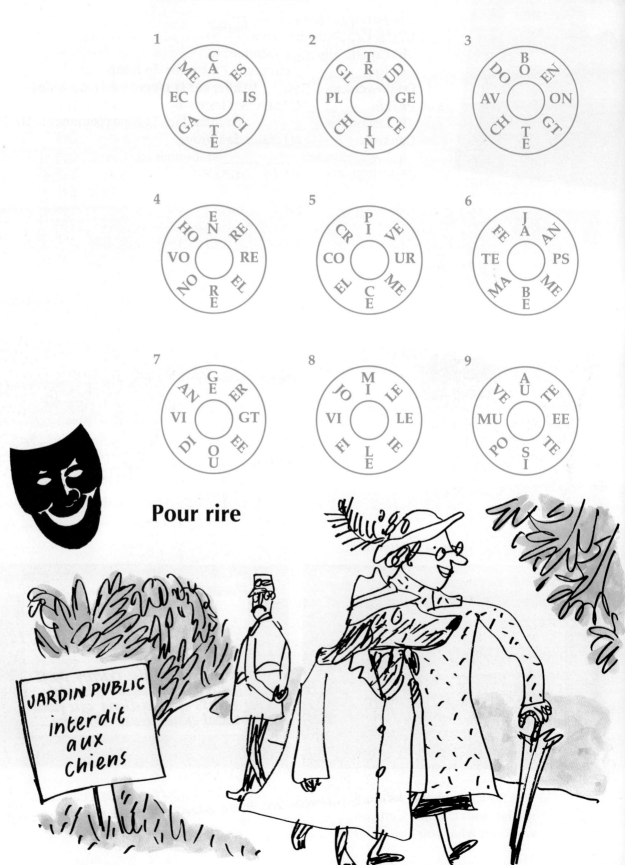

1

ME / C A ES / EC · IS / GA TE CI

2

GL / T R UD / PL · GE / CH IN CE

3

DO / B O EN / AV · ON / CH TE GT

4

HO / E N RE / VO · RE / NO RE EL

5

CR / P I VE / CO · UR / EL CE ME

6

FE / J A AN / TE · PS / MA BE ME

7

AN / G E ER / VI · GT / DI OU EE

8

JO / M I LE / VI · LE / FI LE IE

9

VE / A U TE / MU · EE / PO SI TE

Pour rire

JARDIN PUBLIC
interdit
aux
chiens

A deux: Bon voyage! (page 105)

Partenaire B: employé(e) de la SNCF

Un(e) touriste arrive à ton guichet.
Il/Elle demande des renseignements pour son voyage.
Voici les détails nécessaires:

Destination	Dép.	Arr.	Quai	Prix du billet
PARIS	14H 10	14H 55	1	Aller: 50F Aller-retour: 100F
ROUEN	14H 20	15H 00	4	A: 25F A-R: 50F
CHERBOURG	14H 40	16H 05	2	A: 32F A-R: 64F
MARSEILLE	15H 18	15H 51	4	A: 120F A-R: 240F
DIJON	15H 45	17H 07	3	A: 37F A-R: 74F

A.A. aide la vieille dame à descendre les marches.

En effet, la vieille dame est Margot Maline, déguisée.

Une demi-heure plus tard il rentre au bureau, très content.

```
QYJSR CQNCACQ B'GBGMRQ!
KMG, HC QSGQ ECLGYJC.
TMSQ YSRPCQ, JC 'EPYLB'
NYRPML,Y.Y. CR AC QCPNCLR
QRSNGBC, TMSQ CRCQ
KGLYZJCQ.
```

KyPemr Kyjglc

Peux-tu les aider? Le message est signé 'Margot Maline'.

(Solution: page 157)   151

Fumer...ou ne pas fumer?

Voici un sondage sur le tabac au collège, réalisé par deux des élèves.

Première partie: Ce qu'en pensent les profs...

```
Questions posées aux profs:

1 Etes-vous d'accord avec l'interdiction de la
  cigarette au collège?
2 Vos raisons?

Réponses: (sur 19 profs interrogés)

1 Oui (100%!)
2 Mauvais pour la santé ('Cela démolit la santé',
  'très néfaste à la santé')
  Le respect des autres ('odeur de cigarette
  insupportable, intolérable', 'politesse vis-à-vis
  des autres')
  'N'apporte à l'individu concerné, ni courage, ni
  remède à l'anxiété...et on a beaucoup de
  difficulté à s'en débarrasser!'
```

Deuxième partie: Ce qu'en pensent les élèves de 5^e

```
Questions posées aux élèves:

1 Fumes-tu? (si non, pourquoi?)
2 Depuis combien de temps?
3 Tes parents, sont-ils au courant?
4 Pourquoi fumes-tu:
  a) plaisir?
  b) détente?
  c) besoin?
  d) pour faire comme les autres?
5 Où trouves-tu l'argent?
6 Préfères-tu t'acheter 3 paquets de cigarettes, un
  disque, ou une place de cinéma?

Réponses: (sur 50 élèves interrogés)

1 17 (34%) fument.
  33 (66%) ne fument pas (toujours pour des raisons
  de santé).
2 Là, les réponses sont très variées: 3 mois, 8
  mois, 2 ans, 5 ans.
3 Sur les 17 élèves qui fument, il y en a 11 dont
  les parents sont au courant.
```

4 10 élèves fument par plaisir, 4 par détente, 2
   par besoin et 1 seulement pour faire comme les
   autres.
5 Encore des réponses variées, e.g. argent de
   poche, argent gagné en travaillant un week-end.
6 35 préfèrent une place de cinéma,
   11 préfèrent 3 paquets de cigarettes, et
   4 préfèrent un disque.

Et toi!

... et toi, qu'en penses-tu??

Pour rire

1 Une mouche dit à sa copine:
«Les hommes sont vraiment idiots. Ils
dépensent des fortunes pour faire des
plafonds et ils ne marchent que sur les
planchers!»

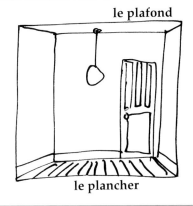

le plafond

le plancher

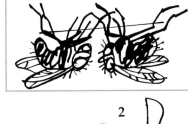

2

Dis donc, où est
le petit?

Le petit? Mais il est...
Zut! J'ai un trou dans
ma poche!

Chanson

Voici une chanson composée par une élève de 5ᵉ.
Les élèves sont contents de rentrer au collège après
les grandes vacances et de revoir leurs professeurs!

Du lundi au samedi
Et le dimanche compris
Nous chantonnons tous en chœur
Notre bonheur
D'aller à la Guérinière
Retrouver Madame BESSIERE
Ses araignées, ses épeires
Et ses fougères.
N'oublions pas nos crayons
Bleus, rouges, jaunes, et le chiffon!
Monsieur DROUET nous attend,
L'air pas content.
Retrouvons Madame LUCAS,
Ses atomes: quel rabat-joie.
Good morning, Mr DAREY,
What are we doing today?

Refrain

Que la vie est belle
Quand on a 11 ans!
Les journées sont telles
Qu'on ne voit pas passer le temps!

Marie-Claude Bourienne

Poésie concrète

Question-Réponse

```
ouèstu                          là
     ouèstu                     làlà
          ouèstu                làlàlà
          ouèstu                làlàlà
          ouèstu                làlàlà
          ouèstu                làlàlà
     ouèstu                     làlàlà
   ouèstu                       làlàlà
ouèstu                          làlà
ouèstu                          là
ouèstu                          là

ouèstu                          là
ouèstu                          làlà
ouèstu                          là
```

Je monte...

```
                                J E
                              E
                            S
                          C
                        A
                      L
                    I
                  E
                R
```

Le mauvais fruit

```
            poi
           poire
          irepoir
         poirepoir
        irepoirep
       repoirepoire
      poirepoirepoir
     epoirepoirepoi
    oirepoirepoirepo
   irepoirepoirepoi
  poirepoireverpoi
   irepoirepoirep
    poirepoirepo
         poire
```

Au secours!

```
droguesdroguesdrogue dr gue
              S   O   S!
```

La mer est dangereuse!

```
mermermermermermermermermermer
mermermermerrequinmermermermer
mermermermermermermermermermer
```

La pollution

Je suis perdu!

TOURNEZ A DROITE
ALLEZ TOUT DROIT
TOURNEZ A GAUCHE

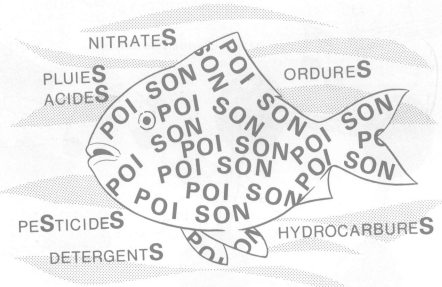

NITRATES
PLUIES
ACIDES
ORDURES
POISON
PESTICIDES
HYDROCARBURES
DETERGENTS

Homme de lettres

```
                    tete
                  tetetete            main
                  tetetete            main
                  tetetete            main
                    tete              bras
                     cc               bras
                     oo               bras
                     uu               bras
        brascorpscorpscorpsbrasbrasbras
        brascorpscorpscorpsbrasbrasbras
      bras        corpscorpscorps
      bras        corpscorpscorps
       bras       corpscorpscorps
        bras      corpscorpscorps
      bras        corpscorpscorps
      bras        corpscorpscorps
      bras        corpscorpscorps
      main        corpscorpscorps
      main        corpscorpscorps
      main        corpscorpscorps
                  jambe        jambe
                  jambe        jambe
                 jambe        jambe
                 jambe        jambe
                 jambe        jambe
                jambe         jambe
                jambe         jambe
                jambe          jambe
            piedpied          piedpied
            piedpied          piedpied
```

Pour rire

– Amélie, peux-tu me dire comment
s'appelle la femelle du hamster?
– Oui monsieur, Amsterdam!

Achille Aricot

```
Solution:   SALUT ESPECES D'IDIOTS!
            MOI, JE SUIS GENIALE.
            VOUS AUTRES, LE 'GRAND' PATRON,
            A.A. ET CE SERPENT STUPIDE,
            VOUS ETES MINABLES.
```

Grammaire

What is grammar?

Grammar is a way of describing language. Different words have different parts to play when we say and write things. Knowing what these parts are, what they're called and how they work can help us to learn a foreign language more easily.

Grammar is a language system or set of 'rules'. Once you know the rules, you can understand and say more things than if you just learn one word at a time.

For example, if you know how -ER verbs work, you can use dozens of verbs by applying the endings rule, and not have to learn each one separately. So if you know, for example, **j'habite**, you can use the **je** parts of **écouter**, **trouver**, **commencer**, **chercher**, etc., etc.

Learning grammar rules is quite hard and not many people enjoy doing it! But if you practise and get to know them, language learning will become much easier.

In this section, the basic grammar rules of French are set out, as simply as possible and with examples to help you understand them.

1 Nouns (Les noms)

Nouns are the names of things, like 'cat', 'house', **frère**, **croissant**. If the name has a capital letter, like 'Julie', 'Bournemouth', **Peugeot**, **la France**, it's called a *proper noun*. Otherwise, it's called a *common noun*.

- To show you understand this, make a list of five proper nouns in English and five in French. Then do the same for common nouns.

2 Masculine and feminine (Masculin et féminin)

Nouns in French are either *masculine* or *feminine*. Masculine and feminine are *genders*. When we use French, it's sometimes difficult for us to remember which gender a noun is:

a Some are obvious: **un garçon** (a boy) is masculine, **une fille** (a girl) is feminine.

b A few nouns can be either: **un/une enfant** (a child), **un/une élève** (a pupil).

c Some groups of nouns – for example, shops – tend to have the same gender: **une boulangerie**, **une pâtisserie**, **une pharmacie**, etc.

d But the gender of most words just has to be remembered: there's no easy way, but the more you use them, the easier it is to know which noun has which gender.

- For practice, make a list of five masculine nouns and five feminine ones. Show which gender they are by putting **le** or **la** in front of each one. Use different ones from the examples above! (If you get really stuck, use the *Vocabulaire français–anglais* at the back of the book.)

3   Plurals (Les pluriels)

Nouns are either *singular* or *plural*. That means that there is either one or more than one. To make a French singular noun into a plural one, you normally add an **-s**, like in English:

le garçon	(the boy)	→	**les garçons**	(the boys)
la maison	(the house)	→	**les maisons**	(the houses)
l'élève	(the pupil)	→	**les élèves**	(the pupils)

- For practice, make these words plural:

le collège	**la banane**
l'enfant	**le professeur**
la voiture	**le salon**

When a singular noun ends in **-s**, **-x** or **-z**, you DON'T add **-s** to make the plural form:

le bras	(the arm)	→	**les bras**	(the arms)
le choix	(the choice)	→	**les choix**	(the choices)
le nez	(the nose)	→	**les nez**	(the noses)

When singular nouns end in **-eau**, **-eu** or **-ou**, most add **-x** to form the plural:

le château	(the castle)	→	**les châteaux**	(the castles)
le jeu	(the game)	→	**les jeux**	(the games)
le bijou	(the jewel)	→	**les bijoux**	(the jewels)

When a singular noun ends in **-al**, the plural usually ends in **-aux**:

le cheval	(the horse)	→	**les chevaux**	(the horses)

159

Note the odd plural form of **l'oeil** (the eye): it's **les yeux** (the eyes). Note also these plurals:

monsieur	→	messieurs
madame	→	mesdames
mademoiselle	→	mesdemoiselles

● What are the plurals of these words?

le cadeau	le chou
le prix	le mois
le journal	le bateau
la souris	le repas
l'oiseau	le morceau

---

4 Articles (Les articles)

a Definite article (l'article défini)
There are four ways of saying 'the' in French:

● **le** with masculine words that are singular (**le garçon**, the boy)

● **la** with feminine words that are singular (**la fille**, the girl)

● **l'** with masculine or feminine words that are singular and begin with a vowel (**a, e, i, o, u**) and usually **h**:

l'arbre (m)	the tree
l'église (f)	the church
l'imperméable (m)	the raincoat
l'oreille (f)	the ear
l'hiver (m)	winter

● **les** with both masculine and feminine nouns when they are plural:

les garçons, les filles, les arbres, les églises, les imperméables, les oreilles, les hivers...

● Using the *Vocabulaire français–anglais*, make a list of any ten nouns that would need **l'** to mean 'the'. Put **(m)** or **(f)** next to them to show which gender they are, and give the meaning, like this:

l'avion (m) the aeroplane

---

b Indefinite article (l'article indéfini)
This is like 'a' or 'an' in English. In French it's **un** for masculine words and **une** for feminine ones:

un oncle	an uncle
une fille	a girl
un arbre	a tree
une église	a church

c Partitive article (l'article partitif)

This is used like 'some' or 'any' in English.

With masculine words it's **du**:

J'achète du lait	I'm buying some milk
Vous avez du vin?	Have you any wine?

With feminine ones it's **de la**:

Il y a de la crème dans le frigo	There's some cream in the fridge
Tu as acheté de la confiture?	Have you bought some jam?

When the word is singular and begins with a vowel, **de l'** is used for both masculine and feminine words:

de l'argent (m)	some/any money
de l'eau (f)	some/any water

With all plurals, **des** is used:

des bananes (f)	some/any bananas
des melons (m)	some/any melons
des abricots (m)	some/any apricots

- To ask for 'some milk' in a French-speaking country, you could say

  'Du lait, s'il vous plaît.'

  In the same way, how would you ask for ... ?

some water	some apples
some jam	some wine
some bananas	some croissants
some cream	some bread

5 Adjectives (Les adjectifs)

Adjectives (like 'small', 'blue', 'interesting', etc.) describe people and things. In French they have to agree with what they are describing.

a Feminines

- Usually an **-e** is added to the adjective to make the feminine form:

le garçon	→	**le petit garçon**
la fille	→	**la petite fille**

- But when the masculine adjective ends in **-e** already, no extra **-e** is added:

  le vélo rouge → **la voiture rouge**

- Adjectives ending in **-er** have the ending **-ère** in the feminine:

premier	→	**première**	(first)
dernier	→	**dernière**	(last)
cher	→	**chère**	(dear)

- Adjectives ending in **-eux** have **-euse** in the feminine:

  | **heureux** | → | **heureuse** | (happy) |
  | **dangereux** | → | **dangereuse** | (dangerous) |

- Some adjectives have a feminine form that has to be remembered separately:

nouveau	→	**nouvelle**	(new)
vieux	→	**vieille**	(old)
blanc	→	**blanche**	(white)
bon	→	**bonne**	(good)
beau	→	**belle**	(fine, beautiful, smart)
quel?	→	**quelle?**	(which?)

- Use some adjectives from the ones above to describe this person:

b Plurals

Plural adjectives are made like plural nouns.

- Add **-s**, unless the adjective ends in **-s** or **-x**:

  | **un vélo bleu** | (a blue bike) | → | **des vélos bleus** | (some blue bikes) |
  | **un vélo gris** | (a grey bike) | → | **des vélos gris** | (some grey bikes) |

- When the adjective ends in **-al**, the plural is usually **-aux**:

  | **le bureau principal** | → | **les bureaux principaux** |
  | (the main office) | | (the main offices) |

c Possessive adjectives

These are like English 'my', 'your', 'his', etc. In French they have to agree with what they describe, as all adjectives do.

	Masculine	**Feminine**	**Plural**
my	mon	ma	mes
your	ton	ta	tes
his/her	son	sa	ses
our	notre		nos
your	votre		vos
their	leur		leurs

Examples:

> **le vélo** is 'the bike', so 'my bike' is **mon vélo**, 'your bike' is **ton vélo**, 'his/her bike' is **son vélo**, etc.

- How would you make **le stylo** mean 'my pen', 'his pen', 'our pen'?

- How would you make **la voiture** mean 'my car', 'our car', 'their car'?

- How would you make **les sandwichs** mean 'your sandwiches', 'her sandwiches', 'our sandwiches'?

---

d Demonstrative adjectives

To say 'this', 'that' and 'those', you have to know whether the word is masculine, feminine or plural:

Masculine	**Feminine**	**Plural**
ce (**cet** before a vowel)	cette	ces

Examples:

ce garçon	this/that boy
cette fille	this/that girl
ces garçons	these/those boys
ces filles	these/those girls
cet élève	this/that boy pupil
cette élève	this/that girl pupil

- Make the following mean 'this/that ...' or 'those ...':

un collège	**une assiette**
une ville	**des bagages**
des sandwichs	**un billet**
une chambre	**une bouteille**
un appartement	**des avions**

---

6   Verbs (les verbes)

The Present tense

a   Regular

You have met two types of regular verbs, -ER and -IR.

- -ER e.g. **parler** (to speak)

je parle	**nous parlons**
tu parles	**vous parlez**
il/elle parle	**ils/elles parlent**

- -IR e.g. **finir** (to finish)

je finis	**nous finissons**
tu finis	**vous finissez**
il/elle finit	**ils/elles finissent**

- From memory, or using the *Vocabulaires*, make a list of ten -ER verbs with their meanings. For example: **parler** (to speak).

- The other most common -IR verb is **choisir** (to choose). Write out the six forms of it, like **finir** above.

---

b   Easy irregular

Some -ER verbs have slightly irregular forms. For example:

- **acheter** (to buy)

j'achète	**nous achetons**
tu achètes	**vous achetez**
il/elle achète	**ils/elles achètent**

- **appeler** (to call)

j'appelle	**nous appelons**
tu appelles	**vous appelez**
il/elle appelle	**ils/elles appellent**

- Can you spot the irregularities in these two verbs?

---

c   Hard irregular

These have to be learnt separately:

aller (to go)	**je vais, tu vas, il/elle va, nous allons, vous allez, ils/elles vont**
avoir (to have)	**j'ai, tu as, il/elle a, nous avons, vous avez, ils/elles ont**
dire (to say, tell)	**je dis, tu dis, il/elle dit, nous disons, vous dites, ils/elles disent**

écrire (to write)	**j'écris, tu écris, il/elle écrit,** **nous écrivons, vous écrivez, ils/elles écrivent**
être (to be)	**je suis, tu es, il/elle est,** **nous sommes, vous êtes, ils/elles sont**
faire (to make, do)	**je fais, tu fais, il/elle fait,** **nous faisons, vous faites, ils/elles font**
mettre (to put, put on)	**je mets, tu mets, il/elle met,** **nous mettons, vous mettez, ils/elles mettent**
ouvrir (to open)	**j'ouvre, tu ouvres, il/elle ouvre,** **nous ouvrons, vous ouvrez, ils/elles ouvrent**
partir (to leave)	**je pars, tu pars, il/elle part,** **nous partons, vous partez, ils/elles partent**
pouvoir (to be able)	**je peux, tu peux, il/elle peut,** **nous pouvons, vous pouvez, ils/elles peuvent**
prendre (to take)	**je prends, tu prends, il/elle prend,** **nous prenons, vous prenez, ils/elles prennent**
venir (to come)	**je viens, tu viens, il/elle vient,** **nous venons, vous venez, ils/elles viennent**
vouloir (to want)	**je veux, tu veux, il/elle veut,** **nous voulons, vous voulez, ils/elles veulent**

Reflexive verbs

The French verbs for 'to get up' and 'to get washed' would appear in English as 'to get yourself up' and 'to get yourself washed'. It's because of this '-self' element that verbs like this are called *reflexive verbs*.

- **se laver** (to get washed)

je me lave	**nous nous lavons**
tu te laves	**vous vous lavez**
il/elle se lave	**ils/elles se lavent**

- **se lever** (to get up)

je me lève	**nous nous levons**
tu te lèves	**vous vous levez**
il/elle se lève	**ils/elles se lèvent**
(note the 4 **è** in this verb)	

Other reflexive verbs you'll need are:

se réveiller	(to wake up)	**se coiffer**	(to comb your hair)
s'habiller	(to get dressed)	**se coucher**	(to go to bed)

- How would you tell someone in French that
  - you wake up at 7 o'clock?
  - you get up at 7.30?
  - you get washed in the bathroom?
  - you get dressed in your bedroom?
  - you go to bed at 10.30?

Future

To say you are going to do something, use **je vais** + a verb. For example:

Je vais manger au restaurant.	I'm going to eat at a restaurant.
Nous allons jouer au tennis.	We're going to play tennis.
Anne va finir ses devoirs.	Anne's going to finish her homework.

- How would you tell someone that
  - you're going to watch television?
  - Philippe's going to buy an ice cream?
  - they're going to go horse-riding?

Perfect

The *Perfect* (**passé composé**) is a past tense: you use it to say what you *have been doing*, *have done* or *did*.

To form it, use a part of **avoir** (**j'ai**, **tu as**, etc.) and the past participle of the main verb.

- Past participles of -ER verbs end in **-é** (**parler** → **parlé, commencer** → **commencé**, etc.).

- Past participles of -IR verbs end in **-i** (**finir** → **fini, choisir** → **choisi**).

- Irregular verbs have irregular past participles. For example:

  faire → **fait**
  prendre → **pris**

- What do these verbs in the Perfect mean?
  - **J'ai parlé français.**
  - **Nous avons joué au squash.**
  - **Ils ont fait de la planche à voile.**
  - **Vous avez choisi un pantalon?**
  - **Tu as nagé dans la mer?**

- How would you tell someone that
  - you've bought a bike?
  - Julie has finished her sandwich?
  - they have visited Paris?
  - you've been listening to the radio?
  - he has taken the train to Dieppe?

Negatives

To make a verb *negative* (for example, to change 'I play football' into 'I don't play football'), use **ne...pas**, like this:

Je joue au football → Je ne joue pas au football.

When the verb starts with a vowel or **h**, **ne** becomes **n'**:

Je n'aime pas les tomates.
Je n'habite pas à Dieppe.

Note the word order with reflexive verbs …

Je ne me lève pas à sept heures le dimanche!

… and verbs in the Perfect tense:

Je n'ai pas joué au tennis.
Il n'a pas écouté le professeur.

- How would you tell someone that
  - you don't play tennis?
  - you don't live in Leicester?
  - you don't like yoghurt?
  - you don't go to bed at 10 o'clock on Saturdays?
  - you didn't watch television?

Je n'aime pas les caniches.

Je n'aime pas les bergers allemands.

Je n'aime pas les chiens méchants...

et je n'aime pas les chiens gentils non plus!

Attention chien gentil!

Vocabulaire classé

1 Les nombres
2 Les jours
3 Les mois
4 Les pays

1 Les nombres

0	zéro	18	dix-huit	71	soixante et onze
1	un	19	dix-neuf	72	soixante-douze
2	deux	20	vingt	80	quatre-vingts
3	trois	21	vingt et un	81	quatre-vingt-un
4	quatre	22	vingt-deux	82	quatre-vingt-deux
5	cinq	30	trente	90	quatre-vingt-dix
6	six	31	trente et un	91	quatre-vingt-onze
7	sept	32	trente-deux	92	quatre-vingt-douze
8	huit	40	quarante	100	cent
9	neuf	41	quarante et un	101	cent un
10	dix	42	quarante-deux	200	deux cents
11	onze	50	cinquante	350	trois cent cinquante
12	douze	51	cinquante et un	999	neuf cent quatre-vingt-dix-neuf
13	treize	52	cinquante-deux		
14	quatorze	60	soixante	1000	mille
15	quinze	61	soixante et un	1035	mille trente-cinq
16	seize	62	soixante-deux	7000	sept mille
17	dix-sept	70	soixante-dix		

2 Les jours

lundi	Monday
mardi	Tuesday
mercredi	Wednesday
jeudi	Thursday
vendredi	Friday
samedi	Saturday
dimanche	Sunday

3 Les mois

janvier	January
février	February
mars	March
avril	April
mai	May
juin	June
juillet	July
août	August
septembre	September
octobre	October
novembre	November
décembre	December

4 Les pays

l'Algérie (f)	Algeria
l'Allemagne (f)	Germany
l'Angleterre (f)	England
l'Autriche (f)	Austria
la Belgique	Belgium
le Danemark	Denmark
l'Ecosse (f)	Scotland
l'Espagne (f)	Spain
la France	France
la Grande-Bretagne	Great Britain
la Grèce	Greece
la Hollande	Holland
l'Irlande (f)	Ireland
l'Italie (f)	Italy
le Luxembourg	Luxembourg
le Maroc	Morocco
la Norvège	Norway
le Pays de Galles	Wales
le Portugal	Portugal
la Suède	Sweden
la Suisse	Switzerland
la Tunisie	Tunisia
la Turquie	Turkey

Vocabulaire français – anglais

d' **abord**   first of all
un **abricot**   apricot
d' **accord**   right! OK, agreed
l' **accueil (m)**   welcome, reception
les **achats (m)**   shopping
acheter   to buy
affectueux (-euse)   affectionate
affranchir   to stamp, put a stamp on
aimer   to like, love
   je n'aime pas tellement   I don't much like
l' **air (m)**   look, looking
une **allée**   pathway
aller   to go
   je vais avoir (13) ans   I'm going to be (13)
un **aller (simple)**   single ticket
un **aller-retour**   return ticket
alors   well, then
un(e) **ami(e)**   friend
amitiés   best wishes, regards
s' **amuser**   to have a good time
un **an**   year
un **anchois**   anchovy
l' **anglais (m)**   English
l' **Angleterre (f)**   England
une **année**   year
une **annonce**   advertisement, announcement
apparaître   to appear
un **appartement**   flat
un **appel**   call
s' **appeler**   to be called
   je m'appelle...   my name is …
apporter   to bring
apprendre   to learn
après   after
l' **après-midi (m)**   afternoon
une **araignée**   spider
l' **argent (m) (de poche)**   (pocket) money
l' **arrêt**   stop(ping)
un **ascenseur**   lift

asseyez-vous   sit down
assez   fairly, quite
une **assiette**   plate
attendre   to wait (for)
attention!   watch out!, be careful!
attiré   attracted
au-dessous   below
aujourd'hui   today
aussi   also
autre   other
avant (de)   before
   en avant   forward
avec   with
une **averse**   shower
un **avion**   aeroplane
   en avion   by plane
   par avion   by airmail
avoir   to have, to be (years old)
   j'ai faim   I'm hungry
   j'ai horreur de...   I hate …
   j'ai mal à (la tête)   (my head) hurts
   j'ai raison   I'm right
   j'ai soif   I'm thirsty

les **bagages (m)**   luggage
se **baigner**   to bathe
le **bain**   bath
le **ballon**   ball
la **barque**   boat
en **bas**   below
le **bateau**   boat
   en bateau   by boat
beau   fine
   il fait beau   it's fine weather
beaucoup (de)   a lot (of)
la **Belgique**   Belgium
le **berger allemand**   alsatian dog
le **besoin**   need
le **beurre**   butter
la **bibliothèque**   library
bientôt   soon
   à bientôt!   see you soon!

la **bienvenue** welcome
la **bière** beer
le(s) **bijou(x)** jewel(s)
le **billet** ticket
blanc(he) white
bleu blue
boire to drink
la **boisson** drink
la **boîte** box, tin, can
    la **boîte aux lettres** postbox
le **bol** bowl
bon(ne) good
le **bonbon** sweet
le **bonheur** happiness
le **bout** end, piece
    au bout de at the end of
la **bouteille** bottle
le **bras** arm
bref in short
le **brouillard** mist, fog
    il y a du brouillard it's misty, foggy
le **bruit** noise
la **bûche** log
le **bûcher** stake
le **bureau** office
    le **bureau des objets trouvés** lost property office
    le **bureau de poste** post office
    le **bureau des renseignements** information office
    le **bureau de tabac** tobacconist's
la **buvette** café

(se) **cacher** to hide
    caché hidden
le **cachet (d'aspirine)** (aspirin) tablet
le(s) **cadeau(x)** present(s)
le **café** café, coffee
    le **café crème/au lait** white coffee
le **cahier** exercise book
    le **cahier de textes** homework notebook
la **caisse** check-out, cash desk
la **calculatrice** calculator
le/la **camarade** friend
la **camionnette** van
la **campagne** country
    à la campagne in/to the country
le **caniche** poodle
le **car** coach
le **cartable** school bag
la **carte** card, map
    la **carte postale** postcard
la **case** square, space

cassé broken
ça va! OK!
ce this, that
ceci this
célèbre famous
ces these, those
cet(te) this, that
chacun(e) each one
la **chaîne** chain
la **chambre** bedroom
    la **chambre d'hôte** bed and breakfast
la **chanson** song
chantonner to sing
le **chapeau** hat
chaque each
le **chariot** trolley
le/la **chat(te)** cat
le(s) **château(x)** castle(s)
chaud hot
chauffé heated
la **chaussée** road
la **chaussette** sock
la **chaussure** shoe
le **chemin** road, way
    le **chemin de fer** railway
la **chemise** shirt
le **chemisier** blouse
cher (chère) dear
chercher to look for
le(s) **cheval (-aux)** horse(s)
la **cheville** ankle
chez at someone's house
    chez moi at home
le/la **chien(ne)** dog
le **chiffon** duster, scrap of paper
le **chiffre** figure
le **chiot** puppy
les **chips (m)** crisps
choisir to choose
le **choix** choice
chut! shh!
le **ciel** sky
cinquième fifth, (school) second form/year
la **circulation** driving, traffic
    la **circulation en vélo** cycle riding
le **citron** lemon
climatisé air conditioned
le **cochon d'Inde** guinea pig
le **coeur** heart
    avoir mal au coeur to feel sick
se **coiffer** to brush/comb your hair
coller to stick

171

combien   how much
   (c'est/ça fait) combien?   how much (does it come to)?
   combien (de)...?   how many … ?
la commande   order
   commander   to order
   comme   as, like
      comme ça   like that
   comment   how, what
le commerçant   shopkeeper
   composter   validate/punch a ticket
   compris   included
   compter   to count
la confiserie   sweet shop
la confiture   jam
   connaître   to know, find out
la consigne   left luggage (office)
      la consigne gratuite   (hypermarket) free use of trolley
   content   pleased
le contrôle   test
   convenable   satisfactory
le/la copain/copine   friend, pal, mate
   cordialement   all the best
le corps   body
le/la correspondant(e)   penfriend
le costume   suit
la côte (de porc)   (pork) chop
à côté de   next to
le cou   neck
se coucher   to go to bed
le couloir   corridor
la cour   yard, playground
au courant   in the know
   courir   to run
le courrier   mail, post, letters
le cours   lesson
   court   short
   coûter   to cost
   couvert   overcast
la cravate   tie
le crayon   pencil
la crème   cream
la crêpe   pancake
les crudités (f)   salads
la cuillerée (de)   spoonful (of)

   dangereux (-euse)   dangerous
   dans   in
se débarrasser de   to get rid of
le déclic   click
   découper   to cut out
   décris   describe

défense de...   it is forbidden to …
   dégoûtant   disgusting
le déjeuner   lunch
      le petit déjeuner   breakfast
   demain   tomorrow
la demande   request
   demander   to ask (for)
le déménagement   moving house
   demi   half
      le demi-tour   about turn, U turn
   démolir   to ruin
la dent   tooth
   dépenser   to spend
   depuis   since, for
   dernier (-ère)   last
   descendre   to go down
le dessin   drawing, art
   dessus   on top, uppermost
la détente   relaxation
   deuxième   second
   devant   in front of
les devoirs (m)   homework
   dîner   to have dinner
se diriger vers   to make for, head for
la discussion   argument
   disparaître   to disappear
      disparu   disappeared
le disque   record
le doigt   finger
   doit, doivent   must
   donc   then
   donner   to give
   dormir   to sleep
le dos   back
la douche   shower
les drogues (f)   drugs
la droite   right
   drôle   funny
la durée   duration, period
   durer   to last

l' eau (minérale) (f)   (mineral) water
      l'eau potable   drinking water
l' Ecosse (f)   Scotland
   écouter   to listen (to)
   écrire   to write
l' éducation physique et sportive (l'EPS) (f)   physical education (PE)
   égaré   strayed, lost
une église   church
un(e) élève   pupil
s' éloigner   to move away
un emblème   logo, emblem

une **émission** programme
un **emplacement** pitch
un **emploi du temps** timetable
une **enceinte** enclosure
enclencher to push in
encore more, again
encore une fois once again
un(e) **enfant** child
enlever to take off
s' **ennuyer** to be bored
ensemble together, overall
un **ensemble** outfit
l'ensemble de the whole of
ensoleillé sunny
ensuite next
entre between
envoyer to send
une **épeire** garden spider
une **épicerie** grocer's
l' **équitation (f)** horse-riding
l' **escalier (m)** stairs
l' **Espagne (f)** Spain
essayer to try (on)
l' **est (m)** east
un **état** state
l' **été (m)** summer
une **étiquette (autocollante)** (self-stick) label
une **étoile** star
eux them
éviter to avoid
un **express** black coffee

la **face** side
face à facing
le **facteur** postman
la **faim** hunger
faire to make, do
fatigant tiring
il **faut** it is necessary
la **femme** wife, woman
la **fenêtre** window
fermer to close
fermé closed
la **fête** festival, holiday, saint's day
la **fille** daughter, girl
le **fils** son
la **fin** end
finir to finish
la **flèche** arrow
la **fleur** flower
la **fois** time, occasion
la **fougère** bracken
frais (fraîche) cool

la **fraise** strawberry
la **framboise** raspberry
le **frère** brother
froid cold
le **fromage** cheese
fumer to smoke
le **(non) fumeur** (non) smoker

gagner to win
gagnant winning
le **garçon** boy, waiter
garder to keep
la **gare** station
le **gâteau** cake
la **gauche** left
gêner to bother, disturb
génial brilliant
le(s) **genou(x)** knee(s)
les **gens (m)** people
gentil(le) nice
la **glace** ice cream
glisser to slide
grand big
gratuit free
grave serious
la **grillade** grill
la **grille** grid
gris grey
gros(se) fat
le **guichet** ticket office

s' **habiller** to dress, get dressed
habiter to live
d' **habitude** usually
heureux (-euse) happy, pleased
hier yesterday
un **hippodrome** race course
l' **hiver (m)** winter
hiverner to (store for) winter
un **homme** man
un **horaire** timetable
un **hôtel de ville** town hall

ici here
une **image** picture
impair odd (number)
un **imperméable** raincoat
n' **importe qui** anyone at all
imprimé printed
instamment earnestly
une **interdiction** ban
interdit forbidden
introduire put in, insert

la **jambe** leg
le **jambon** ham
le **jardin** garden
    le **jardin public** park
jaune yellow
le **jean** (pair of) jeans
le(s) **jeu(x)** game(s)
jeune young
    la **jeune fille** girl, young woman
le **jogging** jogging suit
joli pretty, attractive, nice
jouer to play
le **jour** day
le(s) **journal (-aux)** newspaper(s)
la **journée** day
la **jupe** skirt
jusque/jusqu'à until

le **kiosque à journaux** newspaper stall

là here
le **lac** lake
la **laisse** lead
laisser to leave, let
le **lait** milk
le **lapin** rabbit
large wide
se **laver** to wash, get washed
le/la **lecteur/lectrice** reader
le **légume** vegetable
leur(s) their
se **lever** to get up
libre free
la **ligne** line
    la **grande ligne** main line
lis, lisez read
le **lit** bed
le **littoral** coast
la **livraison** delivery
le **livre** book
loin far
louer to hire
les **lunettes (f)** glasses

ma my
le **magasin** shop
la **main** hand
maintenant now
mais but
la **maison** house
malade ill
manger to eat
le **manteau** (top) coat
la **marche** step

le **marché** market, shopping
marcher to walk
le/la **marcheur/marcheuse** walker
le **mari** husband
le **Maroc** Morocco
la **marque** brand
la **matière** (school) subject
le **matin** morning
mauvais bad
mélangé jumbled, mixed up, mixed
même same
la **menthe** mint
la **mer** sea
    au bord de la mer at the seaside
merci thank you
la **mère** mother
la **merguez** spicy sausage
mes my
mettre to put
midi (m) midday
mieux better
minable pathetic
minuit (m) midnight
la **mode** fashion
moi me
moins minus, less
    ...moins le quart a quarter to …
le **mois** month
mon my
la **montagne** mountain
    à la montagne in/to the mountains
monter to go up
le(s) **morceau(x)** bit(s), piece(s)
mort dead, died
    garage mort storage
le **mot** word
la **moto** motorbike
la **mouche** fly
la **moutarde** mustard
le **moyen** means
moyen(ne) average
le **muguet** lily of the valley
la **myrtille** bilberry

nager to swim
néfaste harmful
la **neige** snow
    il neige it's snowing
neuf new, nine
le **nez** nose
Noël (m) Christmas
noir black
la **noix de coco** coconut

le **nom** (sur)name
se **nommer** to be called
    je me nomme... my name is …
le **nord** north
nos our
la **note** bill, mark
notre our
nouvelle (nouveau) new
nuageux cloudy
la **nuit** night

un **oeuf** egg
l' **oiseau (les oiseaux) (m)** bird(s)
on one, people, they, you
un **oncle** uncle
un **orage** storm
les **ordures (f)** rubbish, waste
une **oreille** ear
ou or
où where
oublier to forget
l' **ouest (m)** west
ouvert open

le **pain** bread
    le pain de mie sandwich loaf
pair even (number)
le **panaché** shandy
le **pansement** bandage, dressing
le **pantalon** (pair of) trousers
le **papier** (piece of) paper
Pâques Easter
par by
parce que because
le **pardessus** (top) coat
le **parfum** flavour, perfume
la **parfumerie** perfume shop
parler to speak
partir to leave
    à partir de from
passer to spend (time)
    passer un film to show a film
le **patron** boss
pauvre poor
le **pays** country, region
la **pêche** fishing, peach
le **pêcheur** fisherman
le **pédalo** pedal boat
la **pelouse** lawn, grassy area
pendant for, during
penser to think
la **pension** board (and lodging), small hotel
perdre to lose

perdu lost
le **père** father
petit small
    le petit déjeuner breakfast
peut-être perhaps
la **pharmacie** chemist's
la **phrase** sentence
la **pièce (de monnaie)** coin
le **pied** foot
le **piéton** pedestrian
la **piscine** swimming pool
la **pistache** pistachio nut
la **place** place, seat, square
le **plafond** ceiling
la **plage** beach
le **plaisir** pleasure
le **plancher** floor
le **plat** dish
    le plat chaud take-away hot meal
il **pleut** it's raining
la **pluie** rain
plusieurs several
la **poche** pocket
le **poids** weight
la **pointure** size (shoes)
la **poire** pear
le **poisson (rouge)** (gold)fish
la **pommade** ointment
la **pomme** apple
le **pont** bridge
porter to wear, carry
poser (une question) to ask (a question)
pour for, in order to
pourquoi why
pousser to push
pouvoir can, to be able
premier (-ère) first
prendre to take, have (meals)
près de near (to)
    tout près (de) very near (to)
le **pressing** dry cleaner's
le **printemps** spring
la **prise** capture
le **prix** price, prize
prochain next
proche (de) near (to)
le **professeur** teacher
promettre to promise
propre clean
puis then

le **quai** platform, riverside street
quand when

quart quarter
    ...et quart a quarter past …
que...! how …!
quel(le) what, which
    quel âge as-tu? how old are you?
    de quelle couleur...? what colour … ?
    quelle heure est-il? what time is it?
    quelle horreur! how awful!
quelque some
quelquefois sometimes
qui who, which
quitter to leave
quoi what

le **rabat-joie** spoilsport
la **raison** reason
   ralentir to slow down
   ramasser to pick up
la **rangée** row
se **rappeler** to remember
la **rayure** stripe
le **récit** story
la **récompense** reward
   reçu(e) received
   recueillir to take note of
   reculer to step back
   récupérer to get back, recover
   regarder to look (at)
la **règle** ruler
le **règlement** rules, regulations
   remercier to thank
le **rempart** rampart
   remplacer to replace
le **rendez-vous** appointment, date
se **rendre** to go
les **renseignements (m)** information
se **renseigner** to make inquiries
la **rentrée (scolaire/des classes)** start of the
    new school year
   rentrer to return (home)
le **repas** meal
   repérer to discover, find out
   répondre to reply, respond
la **réponse** reply
le **requin** shark
   rester to remain
en **retard** late
   retrouver to see again
se **réveiller** to wake up
   revenir to come back, go back
au **revoir** goodbye
les **rillettes (f)** pork potted meat
   rire to laugh

la **robe** dress
   la robe de mariée wedding dress
   rose pink
   rouge red
la **rue** street, road

   sa his, her
le **sac** bag
la **salade composée/mixte** mixed salad
la **salle** room
   la salle à manger dining room
   la salle de bains bathroom
   la salle de séjour living room, lounge
le **salon** lounge
le **saucisson** (slicing) sausage
   sauf except
   savoir to know
au **secours!** help!
la **semaine** week
le **sens** direction
le **sentier** path
   sentir to smell
le **serpent** snake
   serré tight
le **serveur** waiter
la **serveuse** waitress
   ses his/her
   seulement only
   si if
le **siège** seat
   sixième sixth, (school) first form/year
la **soeur** sister
la **soif** thirst
le **soir** evening
le **soleil** sun
   il fait du soleil it's sunny
   son his, her
le **sondage** poll
   sonner to ring
la **sortie** exit
   soudain suddenly
   souhaiter to wish
la **souris** mouse
   sous under
   souvent often
le **sparadrap** sticking plaster
le **stationnement** parking
   stationner to park
le **stylo** pen
le **sud** south
la **Suisse** Switzerland
   suivre to follow
   sur on

sûr sure

    bien sûr of course

le surboum party

    surtout above all

ta your

le (bureau de) tabac tobacconist's

la tablette (de chocolat) bar (of chocolate)

la taille size (person, clothes), height

    quelle taille fais-tu? what size do you take?

la tante aunt

tant pis too bad

tard late

    au plus tard at the latest

la tartelette small individual tart

la tartine slice of bread and butter

la tasse cup

tel(le) such

le temps weather, time

    quel temps fait-il? what's the weather like?

    de temps en temps from time to time, sometimes

tenez here you are

tenu(s) kept

tes your

la tête head

le thé tea

    le thé au lait tea with milk

    le thé au citron tea with lemon

le timbre(-poste) (postage) stamp

le tir shooting

    le tir à l'arc archery

tirer to pull

toi you

tomber to fall

ton your

la tortue tortoise

toujours always

la Toussaint All Saints' Day

tout, tous all, everything

    tout droit straight on

    tous les deux both

le training trainer

la tranche slice

tranquillement peacefully

le travail work

travailler to work

traverser to cross

tremper to dip

très very

le tricot cardigan

le trimestre (school) term

troisième third

trop too

le trou hole

la trousse pencil case

trouver to find

    se trouver to be (situated)

les vacances (f) holidays

le veilleur (de nuit) (night) watchman

le vélo bicycle

le vélomoteur light motorbike

vendre to sell

    à vendre for sale

venir to come

le ventre stomach

le ver worm

vérifier to check

vers about, towards

vert green

la veste jacket

le veston jacket

les vêtements (m) clothes

la viande meat

la vie life

    vieux (vieille) old

la ville town

    un hôtel de ville town hall

le vin wine

voici here is, here are

    me voici here I am

la voie line, track, platform

la voile sailing

    la planche à voile sailboard, windsurfer

voir to see

le/la voisin(e) neighbour

la voiture car, (railway) coach

    en voiture by car

vos your

votre your

vouloir to want (to), like to

    je voudrais I'd like

le voyage journey, trip

    les voyages travel

voyager to travel

le voyageur traveller

vrai true

    vraiment really

la vue view

y there

les yeux (m) eyes

Vocabulaire anglais – français

to be able   **pouvoir**
address   **l'adresse (f)**
aeroplane   **l'avion (m)**
air   **l'air (m)**
   by air   **en avion**
   by airmail   **par avion**
after   **après**
afternoon   **l'après-midi (m)**
age   **l'âge (m)**
   how old are you?   **quel âge as-tu?**
   I'm … years old   **j'ai...ans**
alsatian dog   **le berger allemand**
also   **aussi**
always   **toujours**
and   **et**
animal(s)   **l'animal (m) (les animaux)**
ankle   **la cheville**
apple   **la pomme**
apricot   **l'abricot (m)**
arm   **le bras**
to arrive   **arriver**
art   **le dessin**
aunt   **la tante**

bag   **le sac**
   schoolbag   **le cartable**
baker's   **la boulangerie**
banana   **la banane**
bandage   **le pansement**
bath   **le bain**
to bathe   **se baigner**
bathroom   **la salle de bains**
to be   **être**
beach   **la plage**
because   **parce que**
bed   **le lit**
   to go to bed   **se coucher**
bedroom   **la chambre**
beer   **la bière**
behind   **derrière**
between   **entre**
bicycle   **le vélo**

big   **grand**
biology   **la biologie**
bird(s)   **l'oiseau (m) (les oiseaux)**
black   **noir**
blouse   **le chemisier**
blue   **bleu**
boat   **le bateau**
   by boat   **en bateau**
book   **le livre**
   exercise book   **le cahier**
   homework notebook   **le cahier de textes**
box   **la boîte**
   postbox   **la boîte aux lettres**
boy   **le garçon**
breakfast   **le petit déjeuner**
brother   **le frère**
brown   **brun, marron**
   mid-brown (hair)   **châtain**
but   **mais**
butcher's   **la boucherie**
to buy   **acheter**

cake   **le gâteau**
calculator   **la calculatrice**
to be called   **s'appeler**
car   **la voiture**
   by car   **en voiture**
   car park   **le parking**
card   **la carte**
cash desk   **la caisse**
cassette   **la cassette**
castle   **le château**
cat   **le/la chat(te)**
cereals   **les céréales (f)**
check-out   **la caisse**
cheese   **le fromage**
chemist's   **la pharmacie**
chocolate   **le chocolat**
to choose   **choisir**
church   **l'église (f)**
cinema   **le cinéma**
to close   **fermer**

closed **fermé**
clothes **les vêtements (m)**
cloudy **nuageux**
   it's cloudy **le temps est nuageux**
coat (short) **la veste, le veston**
   raincoat **l'imperméable (m)**
   top coat **le manteau, le pardessus**
coffee **le café**
cold **froid**
to comb your hair **se peigner**
to come **venir**
   to come in **entrer**
   to come home **rentrer**
   to come back **revenir**
country **le pays, la campagne** (countryside)
   in/to the country **à la campagne**
county **le département**
cousin **le/la cousin(e)**
craft, design, technology (CDT) **l'éducation manuelle et technique (l'EMT) (f)**
crocodile **le crocodile**
to cross **traverser**

dancing **la danse**
daughter **la fille**
dictionary **le dictionnaire**
to dine **dîner**
dining room **la salle à manger**
disco **la discothèque**
to dislike **ne pas aimer**
   I don't like **je n'aime pas**
to do **faire**
dog **le/la chien(ne)**
dress **la robe**
to dress **s'habiller**
drink **la boisson**
during **pendant**

ear **l'oreille (f)**
east **l'est (m)**
to eat **manger**
egg **l'oeuf (m)**
end **la fin**
   at the end of (the street) **au bout de (la rue)**
English **(l')anglais**
to enter **entrer**
evening **le soir**
exercise book **le cahier**
eyes **les yeux (m)**

fair (hair) **blond**
family **la famille**
far **loin**
father **le père**

grandfather **le grand-père**
favourite **préféré**
to find **trouver**
fine **beau**
   it's fine weather **il fait beau**
to finish **finir**
first **premier (-ère)**
flat **l'appartement (m)**
flavour **le parfum**
fog **le brouillard**
   it's foggy **il y a du brouillard**
foot **le pied**
football **le football**
for **pour**
forbidden **interdit**
fortnight **deux semaines, quinze jours**
free **gratuit, libre** (room)
French **(le) français**
friend **un(e) ami(e)**
in front of **devant**
fruit **le fruit**
furniture **les meubles (m)**

garage **le garage**
garden **le jardin**
geography **la géographie**
to get up **se lever**
girl **la (jeune) fille**
to give **donner**
glasses **les lunettes (f)**
to go **aller**
   to go down **descendre**
   to go in **entrer**
   to go up **monter**
goldfish **le poisson rouge**
good **bon(ne)**
goodbye **au revoir, salut**
grandfather **le grand-père**
grandmother **la grand-mère**
green **vert**
grey **gris**
grill **la grillade**
grocer's **l'épicerie (f)**
guinea pig **le cochon d'Inde**

hair **les cheveux (m)**
half **demi**
ham **le jambon**
hamster **le hamster**
hand **la main**
happy **content**
hat **le chapeau**
to hate **détester, avoir horreur de**

to have **avoir, prendre** (meals)
head **la tête**
hello **bonjour, salut**
here **ici**
   here is/are **voici**
history **l'histoire (f)**
holidays **les vacances (f)**
horse(s) **le(s) cheval (-aux)**
   horse-riding **l'équitation (f)**
hot **chaud**
house **la maison**
how **comment**
   how are you? **ça va (bien)?**
   how many **combien (de)**
   how much (is it)? **(c'est) combien?**
   how old are you? **quel âge as-tu?**
(I'm) hungry **(j'ai) faim**
husband **le mari**
hypermarket **l'hypermarché (m)**

ice cream **la glace**
ill **malade**
in **dans**

jacket **la veste, le veston**
jam **la confiture**
jeans **le jean**

kitchen **la cuisine**
knee(s) **le(s) genou(x)**

lamp **la lampe**
large **grand, gros**
late **en retard**
lawn **la pelouse**
to leave **quitter**
left **la gauche**
   on the left **à gauche**
leg **la jambe**
lemon **le citron**
lemonade **la limonade**
lesson **le cours**
to like **aimer**
   I don't like **je n'aime pas**
   to like to (do something) **vouloir**
   I'd like … **je voudrais...**
to listen (to) **écouter**
little **petit**
to live (in) **habiter (à)**
living room **la salle de séjour**
loaf **la baguette, le pain**
long **long(ue)**
to look (at) **regarder**
   to look for **chercher**

a lot (of) **beaucoup (de)**
lounge **le salon, la salle de séjour**
to love **aimer, adorer**
lunch **le déjeuner**

to make **faire**
man **l'homme (m)**
map **la carte**
market **le marché**
mathematics **les mathématiques (les maths) (f)**
midday **midi (m)**
midnight **minuit (m)**
milk **le lait**
mint **la menthe**
morning **le matin**
mother **la mère**
   grandmother **la grand-mère**
motorbike **la moto**
mountain **la montagne**
   in/to the mountains **à la montagne**
mouth **la bouche**
museum **le musée**
mushroom **le champignon**
music **la musique**

name **le nom** (surname), **le prénom** (first name)
   my name is … **je m'appelle..., je me nomme...**
near (to) **près (de), proche (de)**
neck **le cou**
newspaper(s) **le(s) journal (-aux)**
next **prochain**
night **la nuit**
north **le nord**
nose **le nez**
now **maintenant**

often **souvent**
ointment **la pommade**
OK **d'accord**
old **vieux (vieille)**
   how old are you? **quel âge as-tu?**
   I'm … years old **j'ai...ans**
   older **aîné**
on **sur**
open **ouvert**
or **ou**
overcast **couvert**

packet **le paquet**
peach **la pêche**
pear **la poire**
pen **le stylo**

pencil   le crayon
   pencil case   la trousse
penfriend   le/la correspondant(e)
perfume   le parfum
   perfume shop   la parfumerie
physical education (PE)   l'éducation physique
   et sportive (l'EPS) (f)
platform   le quai
to play   jouer
please   s'il te/vous plaît (s.v.p.)
poodle   le caniche
postcard   la carte (postale)
post office   la poste
potato   la pomme de terre
to prefer   préférer
present(s)   le(s) cadeau(x)
price   le prix
pullover   le pull(-over)
pupil   un(e) élève
to put   mettre

quarter   le quart
   a quarter to (six)   (6h) moins le quart
quickly   vite
quite   assez

rabbit   le lapin
rain   la pluie
   it's raining   il pleut
raincoat   l'imperméable (m)
raspberry   la framboise
record   le disque
red   rouge
right   la droite
   on the right   à droite
road   la rue, le chemin
room   la chambre (bedroom), la salle
   bathroom   la salle de bains
   dining room   la salle à manger
   living room   la salle de séjour
ruler   la règle

sailing   la voile
salad   la salade
   fruit salad   la salade de fruits
   mixed salad   la salade composée/mixte
sandal   la sandale
sausage (slicing)   le saucisson
school   le collège (secondary school), l'école
   (f)
science   les sciences (f)
sea   la mer
   at/to the seaside   au bord de la mer
second   deuxième

I'm in the second form/year   je suis en
   cinquième
shandy   le panaché
shirt   la chemise
shoe   la chaussure
shop   le magasin, la boutique
short   court
to show   montrer
   to show a film   passer un film
shower   l'averse (f) (weather), la douche
to shut   fermer
   shut   fermé
sick   malade
   I feel sick   j'ai mal au coeur
to sing   chanter
sister   la soeur
size   la taille
   what size do you take?   quelle taille fais-tu?
   (clothes), quelle pointure fais-tu? (shoes)
skirt   la jupe
sky   le ciel
small   petit
snake   le serpent
snow   la neige
   it's snowing   il neige
sock   la chaussette
son   le fils
soon   bientôt
south   le sud
to speak   parler
to spend (the afternoon)   passer (l'après-midi)
stamp   le timbre(-poste)
station   la gare
sticking plaster   le sparadrap
stomach   le ventre
storm   l'orage (m)
straight on   tout droit
strawberry   la fraise
street   la rue
subject (at school)   la matière
suit   le costume
summer   l'été (m)
   in summer   en été
sun   le soleil
   it's sunny   il fait du soleil
supermarket   le supermarché
sweet   le bonbon
   sweet shop   la confiserie
to swim   nager
swimming pool   la piscine

tail   la queue
to take   prendre

to talk **parler**
tall **grand**
tea **le thé**
teacher **le professeur**
tee-shirt **le tee-shirt**
television **la télé(vision)**
tennis **le tennis**
thank you **merci**
there is/are **il y a**
third **troisième**
(I'm) thirsty **(j'ai) soif**
ticket **le billet**
   single ticket **l'aller (m)**
   return ticket **l'aller-retour (m)**
   ticket office **le guichet**
tie **la cravate**
tight **serré**
time **l'heure (f)**
   at what time … ? **à quelle heure...?**
   what time is it? **quelle heure est-il?**
timetable **l'emploi du temps (m)** (school),
   l'horaire (m) (station)
tin **la boîte**
tobacconist's **le bureau de tabac**
today **aujourd'hui**
tomorrow **demain**
too **trop**
   too hot/cold **trop chaud/froid**
   too many people **trop de monde**
tooth **la dent**
tortoise **la tortue**
tourist **le/la touriste**
   tourist office **l'office de tourisme (m)**
town **la ville**
   town hall **l'hôtel de ville (m)**
   (to go) to town **(aller) en ville**

train **le train**
   by train **par le train**
trousers **le pantalon**
to turn **tourner**

uncle **l'oncle (m)**
usually **d'habitude**

vegetable **le légume**
very **très**
village **le village**
to visit **visiter**

waiter **le garçon, le serveur**
waitress **la serveuse**
to wake up **(se) réveiller**
to want (to) **vouloir**
to wash **(se) laver**
to wear **porter**
weather **le temps**
   what's the weather like? **quel temps fait-il?**
week **la semaine**
west **l'ouest (m)**
when **quand**
where **où**
white **blanc(he)**
why **pourquoi**
wide **large**
wife **la femme**
windsurfing **la planche à voile**
wine **le vin**
with **avec**
woman **la femme**

yellow **jaune**
yesterday **hier**
young **jeune**

Acknowledgements

The Authors and Publishers gratefully acknowledge the help they have received from the following:

Provision of materials: Muriel Cécille, Annie Fatet, Valérie Harkness, Bob Holland, Gisèle Leedham, Jean-Marc Rougeon, John Wren, Office de Tourisme de Dieppe, Office de Tourisme de Rouen, the Collège La Guérinière in Caen and most particularly Madame M. Massot and the pupils of class 5e 2.

Revision of draft material:

Stephen Burnett, Head of Languages, Abraham Darby School, Telford
David Richardson, Head of Languages, Woodkirk High School, Leeds
Dennis Rudd, Head of Languages, Trinity School, Carlisle.

Revision of the typescript: Muriel Cécille and Madeleine Bender.

The illustrations are by Tim Archbold, Jane Cheswright, Rebecca Gryspeerdt, Claire James and Steve Noon.

The photographs are by the authors and Frances Webb except:
CRT Normandie: Rouen, place du Vieux Marché and Grande Rue
(p. 103), John Wren: Belgian nationality plate (p. 126, photo g).

The Authors and Publishers are grateful to the following for permission to reproduce copyright material:

Maroquiniers de Paris: advertisement (p. 7), Michelin: map of Caen from their map number 231 1988/89 edition (p. 8), Kellogg's produits alimentaires: Frosti, Miel pops and Cornflakes packets (p. 22), The Nestlé Co. Ltd: Shreddies packet, reproduced with the kind permission of the trademark owners (p. 22), Effem GmbH: Brekkies packet (p. 22), Marks and Spencer: clothing labels (p. 37), Galeries Lafayette: brochure (p. 39), Clichés Estel – Blois: postcards of Dieppe (pp. 83 & 121), Office de Tourisme de Dieppe: leaflets (pp. 84 & 90), National Museum of Wales, Cardiff: Rouen Cathedral by Monet (p. 103), SNCF: Guide pratique du voyageur – text (p. 106), Climat de France SARL: logo (p. 127) and sign (p. 129). 'Le mauvais fruit' (p. 156) is adapted from 'Apfel' by Reinhard Dohl in *Anspiel*, Inter Nationes.